Diary of an Unforgettable Season

Steve Snapp

TRIUMPH
B O O K S

Triumph Books and colophon are registered trademarks of Random House, Inc.

Library of Congress Cataloging-in-Publication Data

Snapp, Steve, 1945–
    Diary of an unforgettable season / Steve Snapp.
        p. cm.
    ISBN-13: 978-1-57243-978-8
    ISBN-10: 1-57243-978-5
        1. Ohio State Buckeyes (Football team) 2. Ohio State University—Football. 3. Snapp, Steve, 1945—Diaries. I. Title.

    GV958.O35S53 2007
    796.332'630977157—dc22

                                        2007022656

This book is available in quantity at special discounts for your group or organization. For further information, contact:

Triumph Books
542 South Dearborn Street
Suite 750
Chicago, Illinois 60605
(312) 939-3330
Fax (312) 663-3557

Printed in U.S.A.

ISBN: 978-1-57243-978-8

Design by Amy Carter

All photos courtesy of AP/Wide World Photos unless otherwise indicated.

Dedication

This book is dedicated to the seniors on the 2006 Ohio State football team. Thanks for a magical year, one I will always remember. My thanks, too, to my former boss Marv Homan, a mentor, a friend, and a true gentleman in every sense of the word.

Contents

Foreword

This is the story of the 2006 Ohio State football family.

It is the story of more than 100 football players and 10 full-time coaches who put their individual goals aside to achieve a singleness of purpose. It is the story of 19 seniors who never—not during the 6:00 AM winter workouts, not in spring practice as they were developing a personality, not during the rugged two-a-days of fall camp, and certainly not during the grind of a 12-week season—lost their focus or commitment to one another. And it is the story of a group of young men who became One in every way—mentally, physically, and spiritually.

Prior to the 2006 season, all of us, coaches and players alike, settled on two goals: winning the Big Ten title and capturing the national championship. While our second goal went unfulfilled against an extremely talented Florida team, I am enormously proud of what these student-athletes accomplished in the classroom, on the football field, and in the community. This was a team in every sense of the word.

Thanks to the tireless work of Steve Snapp, the pages that follow will give you a glimpse into the inner workings of the 2006 Buckeyes team. In the long and storied history of The Ohio State University, I cannot think of a team more deserving of such a thorough chronicling. It was truly an unforgettable season.

Go Bucks!

— Jim Tressel

Introduction

When it comes to Ohio State football, expectations are always high. The 2006 season was no exception. The Buckeyes were coming off a 10–2 campaign in 2005 that included seven straight wins, culminating in a victory over Michigan in Ann Arbor followed by a thrashing of Notre Dame in the Fiesta Bowl. The Big Ten co-champion Buckeyes were arguably the nation's best college football team at the end of the year. In reality, their fourth-place finish in the polls really did not give head coach Jim Tressel's players the credit they deserved.

But as Tressel often says, "You get as your works deserve," and the Buckeyes had lost two games early, all but eliminating themselves from the national championship hunt.

Almost before the Buckeyes arrived back in Columbus following their win over Notre Dame, their fans were thinking ahead to the 2006 campaign.

With Heisman Trophy candidate Troy Smith at the controls and a cast of holdovers that included the receiving tandem of Ted Ginn Jr. and Anthony Gonzalez as well as tailback Antonio Pittman, there would be plenty of firepower on offense. Additionally, the offensive line appeared to be the deepest and most talented in Tressel's six-year stay with the Buckeyes.

The defense, to be sure, had lost a wealth of talent, including the outstanding linebacking trio of All-Americans A.J. Hawk, Bobby Carpenter, and Anthony Schlegel, as well as all four starters in the secondary. But at Ohio State you don't rebuild, you reload. Every good Ohio State fan knows that. Besides, in the Tressel revolving-door system, a lot of players see action during the course of the year. Nine starters were gone, but the cupboard was far from bare. If the offense could shoulder the majority of the load early, the defense would come around.

If this team could get through a brutal September that included road games at Texas and Iowa, there was no reason it could not contend for the national championship, which, incidentally, was in Phoenix. If the Buckeyes were to get there it would be their fourth trip to the Valley of the Sun in five years.

And the fans were right: it would turn out to be a memorable season, filled with highlights and special memories.

Here is how the season unfolded.

1

Hope Springs Eternal

Spring practice opens today. In many ways it is the time of year that Jim Tressel enjoys most, because it is a time for teaching. Whenever the Buckeye football coach is queried as to what profession he would be in if he were not a coach, he always replies, "I would be a teacher; teaching is what I really enjoy."

Tressel is the consummate teacher. His meetings are like classrooms and his practices are like labs in which his players put into practice what he has taught them. When practice is over, it is back to the classroom to review the day's subject matter.

Tressel and his staff need to be on their "A" game this spring. Nine starters from what was arguably the best defense in the nation are gone, including the trio of Hawk, Carpenter, and Schlegel. On offense, left guard Robbie Sims, center Nick Mangold, and split end Santonio Holmes, all of whom had been three-year starters, need to be replaced. Additionally, kicker Josh Huston, who tied a school record with five field goals against Texas and earned All–Big Ten honors, has graduated, leaving a giant question mark in the place-kicking department.

But while the losses are significant, the Buckeyes are not short on talent. Tressel's goal is to develop that talent during the 15 spring practices allotted by the NCAA.

Saturday, April 1

During the traditional "hoot and holler" drill on the first day of pads, true freshman running back Chris "Beanie" Wells flattened a veteran senior defender in a show of raw power. In the drill, an offensive player gets three chances to go 10 yards. Beanie only needed one try. It is evident that the former *USA Today* All-American is the real deal.

The 6'1", 225-pound Wells was one of three true freshmen to enroll early. The other two are linebacker Ross Homan and defensive back Kurt Coleman.

Saturday, April 8

The Buckeyes held their jersey scrimmage, pitting the offense against the defense. The winning unit will wear the home scarlet-colored jerseys through the remainder of spring ball and into fall practice. The losers will be clad in the white away jerseys until they get a chance to redeem themselves in the fall.

Much of the media discussion leading into the spring was about the inexperience of the defense. In stark contrast to recent years, it appears that early on at least, the offense will have the edge.

On this day, though, the defense was having none of that. Jim Heacock's young, but undeniably talented and surprisingly fast defensive unit forced five turnovers and came away with a 69–68 victory, using a unique scoring system that Jim Tressel's father, the late Lee Tressel, used when he coached at Baldwin-Wallace College.

Several young players stood out on the defensive side of the ball, including, but not limited to, linebacker Ross Homan, safety Anderson Russell, defensive end Lawrence Wilson, and linebacker James Laurinaitis.

"You can tell these young guys want to be good and uphold the tradition of excellent Ohio State defense," said Tressel, who deep down inside probably did not mind the outcome. "This will help their confidence."

The defense won the scarlet jerseys even though tackle Quinn Pitcock, one of just two returning starters on that side of the ball, did not play.

The offense was without two of its top linemen, right tackle Kirk Barton and Doug Datish, who, after starting at guard in 2004 and 2005, is sliding over to center this fall as a replacement for departed All-American Nick Mangold.

But Troy Smith would not use that as an excuse.

"We got our butts whipped and I don't like that feeling, whether it is in a practice or a scrimmage," he said.

The scrimmage came down to a 58-yard field-goal attempt by Ryan Pretorius on the final play of the game. When the defense blocked the kick, it was worth one point and broke a 68–all tie.

Friday, April 14

Football is a violent game. Over the years, players have gotten bigger, stronger, and faster. Sometimes the collisions on the field are unnerving.

Ohio State has been fortunate to have never suffered a fatality in either a practice or a game. And up until this spring, the Buckeyes had never had a serious neck or spinal cord injury.

That changed during a scrimmage in Ohio Stadium today.

Walk-on Tyson Gentry, who made the squad as a punter and for the first time this spring was also working at wide receiver, was running a square-in when he was tackled by freshman defensive back Kurt Coleman. The hit was clean and was not one of those bone-jarring tackles that make fans cringe. But when the two players hit the ground, Tyson was completely motionless. Everyone in the stadium—the coaches; the players; the doctors and trainers; and the family members in the stands, including his parents, Bob and Gloria Gentry—knew it was serious.

As the team doctors and the Gentry family hurried to his side, the training staff called 911.

All the while there was an eerie hush in the stadium. Everyone was praying and thinking, "Come on Tyson, just move something." Although Tyson was conscious and talking the entire time, there was no movement.

Once the ambulance left for the Ohio State medical center, Tressel called the team together. After a brief prayer, the coach canceled practice and sent the team home for the Easter holiday.

Tressel immediately headed to the hospital along with several members of the team. Gentry had suffered a fracture of the C4 vertebra. He had surgery tonight to fuse the vertebra.

Thursday, April 20

The Kick Scrimmage. The kicking game has always played an important role in the success of Tressel's teams, both in his 15 years at Youngstown State, where he won four Division I-AA national championships, and at Ohio State, where in just his second year he captured the 2002 national championship.

Tressel, who calls the punt "the most important play in football," has had a remarkable string of kickers since coming to Ohio State.

Mike Nugent was a three-year starter at place-kicker during the 2002, 2003, and 2004 seasons, and garnered first-team All-America honors in '02 and again in '04. In the latter season he also won the Lou Groza Award as the nation's top place-kicker. In 2005, Josh Huston took over Nugent's duties and the Buckeyes never missed a beat.

Huston graduated following the 2005 season. The job is wide open.

Ryan Pretorius, a 27-year-old sophomore from Durban, South Africa, and Aaron Pettrey, a redshirt freshman from Raceland, Kentucky, are competing for the position. Both are untested, although Pretorius appeared in two games in 2005.

Tressel hoped to get an answer in the kick scrimmage, but with Pretorius hitting six of seven tries and Pettrey drilling a 60-yarder to give the Gray team a 28–27 win, the Buckeyes coach heads into the fall still looking for a clear-cut number one.

"Looks like we have a pretty good battle going on," he said. "We will just have to wait until the fall and see what happens."

Saturday, April 22

The public got its first look at the team at the annual Scarlet and Gray Game in Ohio Stadium. The spring game routinely attracts numbers in excess of 30,000, but on this day that figure more than doubled with an announced crowd of 63,649, not counting children ages six and under. The game was broadcast by WBNS Radio and televised locally and around the state by WBNS-TV and the Ohio News Network.

Wide receiver Roy Hall's catch between two defenders wasn't enough to lead his team to victory in the annual Scarlet and Gray game during spring practice.

The game was won by the Scarlet team as Smith directed a nine-play, 80-yard touchdown drive on his team's opening possession. Smith completed four passes on the march for 62 yards. Erik Haw scored the only touchdown of the day on a four-yard run.

The Scarlet team scored five points in the second quarter on a safety and a 38-yard field goal by Ryan Pretorius to complete the scoring.

Freshman Beanie Wells gained 48 yards on the ground for the Scarlet, and Brian Hartline had seven receptions for

88 yards to lead all receivers. Maurice Wells (34 yards rushing) and Roy Hall (five catches for 66 yards) led the Gray.

Spring practice was over.

"We have had a good winter conditioning program and a good spring," said Tressel, addressing the media after the game. "What is most important now is how hard our players work during the summer leading up to fall camp."

Outside the Lines

Five Ohio State players were taken in the first round of the NFL draft. Not surprisingly, linebacker A.J. Hawk was the first Buckeye taken, going to the Green Bay Packers with the fifth overall pick—a perfect fit. Hard-hitting safety Donte Whitner, to the surprise of many, was the next player chosen, going to Buffalo with the eighth pick. Linebacker Bobby Carpenter went to Dallas (No. 18), followed by Santonio Holmes to the Pittsburgh Steelers (No. 25), and center Nick Mangold to the New York Jets (No. 29). Overall, the Buckeyes had nine players taken.

The Heisman Trophy is the most prestigious individual award in college football. Named for legendary coach John W. Heisman, it was established in 1935 and is awarded each December to the "outstanding player in college football."

Prior to the terrorist attack on New York City in 2001, the trophy was presented at the Downtown Athletic Club, a cathedral to football located on the Lower East Side. Now the presentation is held in midtown Manhattan.

Heading into the 2006 season, six Ohio State players have won the Heisman, including Archie Griffin, who in 1975 became the first two-time winner of the prestigious award. Forty years later, he is still the only person to have bookend Heismans sitting in his trophy room.

Each spring, the Athletics Communications staff meets with the head coach and develops a game plan for promoting players for postseason honors. In my opinion, and in Coach Tressel's, All-America honors and individual awards should be won through performance on the football field. But we both concede that exposure is necessary to ensure that your players are not overlooked.

How to promote has changed dramatically over the years.

My first football season at Ohio State was 1972. It was the beginning of a truly golden era of football in which the Buckeyes won four Big Ten titles, played in a still unprecedented four Rose Bowls, and compiled an overall record of 40–5–1. Names like Gradishar, Hicks, Skladany, DeCree, Colzie, and Griffin dotted the roster. All earned first-team All-America honors. Hicks won the Outland and Lombardi Awards and finished second in the Heisman voting as a senior in 1973. Griffin, of course, remains to this day one of the most celebrated players in college football history.

Back then, there were no major promotional campaigns for players. In the days before television deregulation, teams were limited to two appearances a year. Ohio State always had two, one of which was the annual regular-season finale with Michigan. If the Buckeyes fared well in those televised games, and they usually did, they were going to get their fair share of All-Americans.

Additionally, Woody Hayes was one of the most dominant personalities of his time. At his weekly press conferences, Woody, who could be extremely persuasive, never missed a chance to promote his players.

Griffin was already in the headlines every Sunday because of his streak of consecutive 100-yard rushing games Hayes's effusive praise of his star running back was icing on the cake. Once Archie won the first Heisman, all the talk the following season centered around whether he would become the first repeat winner. Griffin responded with another outstanding year as a senior and led the Buckeyes to an unbeaten regular season. Hayes continued to praise the diminutive running back, and Griffin made football history that December by becoming the first two-time Heisman winner.

By the time Eddie George won his Heisman in 1995, promotion was in full bloom. Sports information directors across the country were promoting their awards candidates in a variety of ways, including mailings, billboards, and gimmickry.

To help promote Eddie, we used a series of what we believed to be creative postcards that were mailed out weekly to members of the Football Writers of America. The picture on the front changed each week, as did the information on the back, which included updated stats, any records set, and quotes from opposing coaches and players.

Eddie won the Heisman, but not because of those postcards. He ran for 1,927 yards that year and had his biggest games on national television. Still, I would like to think we helped a little.

The following year, Ohio State's best football player was junior offensive tackle Orlando Pace. Pace was probably the best football player in the country, but realistically we knew winning the Heisman would be a long shot for him. Since offensive linemen don't have a lot of stats, we came up with a refrigerator magnet shaped like a stack of pancakes with Pace's name and a crown on top of it. Our not-so-subtle message was that Orlando Pace was king of the pancake block—which is when the offensive lineman deposits the defender across from him directly on his backside. And it was not an exaggeration; nobody did it better than Pace, who has gone on to become one of the dominant linemen in the NFL.

Pace did not win the Heisman but he did finish fourth. Had he stayed for his senior year, who knows?

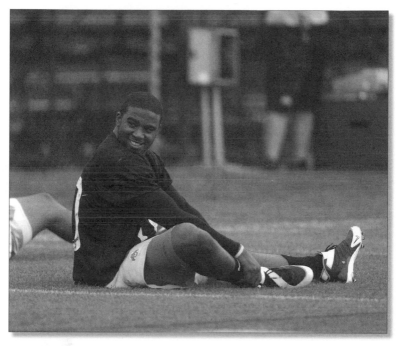

Quarterback Troy Smith entered the 2006 season as the un-
questioned leader of a talented Ohio State football team.

Thankfully, the days of the gimmicky promotion seem
to have gone by the wayside. Still, as I noted earlier, it is
necessary to keep your athlete, or athletes, in the spotlight.

Entering this season, Ohio State appears to have two legitimate Heisman contenders in quarterback Troy Smith and
flanker and return specialist Ted Ginn Jr. Both are coming off
strong showings last year and both play for a team expected
to be in the hunt for the national title. Smith outplayed his

Notre Dame counterpart, Brady Quinn, in the Fiesta Bowl, and has quarterbacked the Buckeyes to consecutive wins over Michigan. Ginn, who had nine catches at Michigan and eight against the Irish in the Fiesta Bowl, is considered one of the most electrifying players in college football.

There was a time when two candidates from a team was one candidate too many. The conventional wisdom was that if you had two candidates, you really did not have any because they would split the vote and someone else would win. A prime example of that was in 1973 when Ohio State had three players—John Hicks, Archie Griffin, and Randy Gradishar—finish in the top six of the Heisman voting. Together, they had more votes than winner John Cappelletti of Penn State.

But the University of Southern California blew that theory out of the water in 2005 by promoting both junior running back Reggie Bush and senior quarterback Matt Leinart. Bush won the award. Leinart, who had won it in 2004, finished third behind Bush and Texas quarterback Vince Young.

This season the coaches have decided to promote both Smith and Ginn for the Heisman Trophy. The voters will be inundated with information on both players, and the choice will be theirs to make.

The plan is simple. First we will try to get them as much preseason coverage as possible. That should be easy. Most magazines and major publications, including *Sports Illustrated*,

Street & Smith, Athlon, ESPN The Magazine, and *USA Today,* come to us seeking either interviews or cover shoots.

Next, we will send out a preseason mailer to the 700 or so members of the Football Writers of America. A Web page will be set up for both players, and a weekly teleconference will afford the national media the opportunity to call in and interview them. Associate SID Dan Wallenberg is going to oversee the Web page and teleconference.

We also plan to send out another mailer the first week of November 2006. Diana Sabau, our director of publications, came up with the idea—a card on bronze-colored stock that features a raised replica of the Heisman Trophy. Across the top it will read: The Ohio State University. Down the sides will be the names of Ohio State's six Heisman winners. No mention is made of Troy or Ted. We hope it will be a gentle reminder at voting time.

We have a plan. Now we just have to wait and see how the season plays out.

Tuesday, May 16

The Big Ten released its early-season television schedule. The Buckeyes, as expected, will play Texas in prime time on September 9. Additionally, OSU's game at Iowa on September 30 will be played after dark. ABC will televise both games nationally and ESPN's *College GameDay* is scheduled to be at both sites.

Thursday, May 18

Director of athletics Eugene Smith announced that coach Jim Tressel had signed a new contract that will take him through the 2012 season. "Jim Tressel is one of the finest coaches in the country and we felt it was important to get him near the top nationally in terms of compensation," said Smith. "This agreement does that and allows us to keep one of the best coaches in America at Ohio State."

Wednesday, May 24

Wheelchair-bound Tyson Gentry attended the Ohio State Scholar-Athlete Dinner. Eugene Smith introduced him to a standing ovation. It was Gentry's first public appearance since his accident.

Tyson has made steady progress, gradually regaining movement in the upper body. His lower body has been slower to respond, but he and his family are undaunted.

Friday, May 26

I received a phone call from Jim Bollman, our offensive co-ordinator, tonight.

"Hey Bolls, what's up?" I asked.

"I wanted to give you a call and let you know what was happening with me just in case you didn't know," he said.

"I have no idea what you are talking about," I replied.

"Well, I am over here at University Hospital and I am going to have open-heart surgery tomorrow," he explained. "I was on the road recruiting earlier in the week and just didn't feel good, so I came home and saw the doctor. They did some preliminary tests and decided to do the surgery sooner rather than later. So we are doing it tomorrow."

Saturday, May 27

Bollman had open-heart surgery and came through with flying colors.

3

Great Expectations

Troy Smith received his undergraduate degree in communication and accomplished his goal of graduating in four years. "That was huge for me," he said. "It was one of the earliest goals I set when I came to Ohio State."

The Big Ten and ABC announced the Ohio State–Michigan game will kick off at 3:30 PM on November 18. That will be the latest kickoff in the history of the storied rivalry. Since the deregulation of television, the game has traditionally started at noon, although there has been an occasional 1:00 PM start. Suffice it to say, fans from both schools did not take kindly to the change. There are some things that you just don't mess with and The Game falls into that category. From the Ohio State coaches' and players' perspectives, however, it really is not a big deal. The Buckeyes are used to playing televised games at 3:30. That is the price you pay for success. And by making this move, stations on the West Coast will be able to clear the broadcast.

Expectations were sky-high for Ohio State in 2006, and head coach Jim Tressel had the Buckeyes focused on winning another national championship.

Friday, June 16

Quarterbacks coach Joe Daniels experienced discomfort in his chest while at the office. A visit to the emergency room confirmed that he had suffered a mild heart attack. Doctors determined it would not be necessary to do open-heart surgery. That was the good news. Unfortunately, bad news followed. While doing some follow-up testing, the doctors discovered a malignant tumor near Joe's kidney. He had been feeling fine and had no idea anything was wrong. Daniels is beginning treatment immediately.

Monday, June 19

Eric Lichter is named Ohio State's new strength and conditioning coach. Lichter, whose official title is Director of Football Performance, has been in private business in northeast Ohio and has successfully tutored a number of standouts, including LeBron James. He is the son of Linda Lichter-Witter, who is the Buckeyes' synchronized swimming coach. Lichter replaced Allan Johnson, who resigned in May to go into private business.

Wednesday, July 12

A writer from *Sports Illustrated* called to say Ohio State will be number one in its preseason issue. They need to talk to Tressel and set up a cover shot. Great publicity if you don't believe in jinxes.

Friday, July 28

This time the call was from Tom O'Toole, the sports editor at *USA Today*. The Buckeyes will be their number one preseason pick and they would like to meet with Tressel on the Q.T. the following week at the Big Ten Kickoff Luncheon in Chicago.

Tuesday, August 1

The unofficial start of the football season for Big Ten schools is the Big Ten Kickoff Luncheon in Chicago. The brainchild of former Big Ten commissioner Wayne Duke, the two-day extravaganza brings together all 11 head coaches, players from each school, 350 or so members of the national media, bowl reps, and about 1,900 fans who attend the actual luncheon on the second day. As the old saying goes, "You can't buy that kind of publicity." Other conferences have tried to duplicate it, but with little or no luck. There is just something special about football in the Midwest.

The first Kickoff Luncheon was held in 1973. When Wayne Duke suggested it, a lot of people had their doubts. We already had a pretty good system in place for previewing the season: the Skywriters—a group of touring writers from each Big Ten city who flew via charter from campus to campus and spent a day there interviewing the head coach and players. It was 10 days of constant coverage. How could it get better than that? The Kickoff Luncheon was only two days, everyone reasoned. It didn't compare. But they were wrong! And over the years, it has become the premier preview event in college football.

Tressel and three Ohio State players—Smith, Datish, and Pitcock—arrived in Chicago early and checked in at the Hyatt Regency. The three seniors are scheduled to meet with an assortment of print and electronic media during the next 36 hours.

Tressel's first obligation was to meet with the print media. Each coach has 15 minutes for an opening statement and follow-up questions. That doesn't seem like a long time, but it works.

Before heading to his next scheduled event, Tressel got together with Mike Dodd from *USA Today* and discussed his thoughts on being number one.

"We are honored," he said. "I think it shows how much respect people have for Ohio State. After all, we lost nine starters on defense and two first-round draft picks on offense.

"Of course, our goal is to be number one at the end of the season. To do that we are going to have to get better each and every day through fall camp and once the season starts. That is our challenge as a football team."

The media in attendance at the event selected Ohio State as the preseason favorite to win the Big Ten title. Michigan was picked second and Iowa third. Troy Smith gets the nod as Preseason Offensive Player of the Year.

Wednesday, August 2

The luncheon was held before a packed house of nearly 1,700 in the Grand Ballroom at the Hyatt. Prior to the event the players and coaches met with the media from 8:00 AM to 10:00 AM in an informal setting that allowed the media to roam from table to table to get their interviews.

At 10:00 the players and coaches moved to an area adjacent to the Grand Ballroom for an hour-long autograph session. Smith was everyone's favorite, and even though he signed continuously during the allotted time, a number of fans went away disappointed.

The luncheon was emceed by ABC's Mark Jones. Bowl reps and other dignitaries were introduced, and there was a very moving video of the late Randy Walker, the Northwestern coach who passed away unexpectedly in July.

Each of the coaches spoke briefly, free to deliver the message of their choice in their allotted three minutes. If there was a common theme, it was that they were all anxious to get started.

Friday, August 4

The *USA Today* coaches' poll has been released. As luck would have it, this is the same day *Sports Illustrated* scheduled its photo shoot with Smith, Downing, and Datish, so all three were available to meet with members of the local media who were looking for a reaction to the poll.

All three players were excited but humble. They know there is still a long way to go. Texas is second in the poll. The two teams meet September 9 in Austin.

Sunday, August 6

Fall camp starts as the players check in at the team hotel, The University Plaza, and then bus to the Woody Hayes Athletics Center for the first of many meetings. The opener, against Northern Illinois, is 27 days away.

Monday, August 7

The first practice of the new season. Per NCAA rules, players are required to spend two days in helmets and two days in shells (helmets and shoulder pads) before donning full gear and being allowed to hit. The players are kept busy the first few days with meetings and practice and then more meetings. Jim Bollman is back, 30 pounds lighter but cantankerous as ever. Joe Daniels was there too. Seeing the two of them run out on the field was special.

Tuesday, August 8

The Athletics Communications staff and three members of the local media met with the team in an hour-long media training seminar designed to prepare the players for the intense media coverage they receive at Ohio State. In past years, outside firms have been used, but the decision was made to keep it in-house this year. The players seemed very receptive both to our presentation and to the presentation of the media.

Wednesday, August 9

Rainy weather forced the team to move inside the Woody Hayes Athletics Center for the first portion of Picture Day. Individual pictures were taken on the indoor practice field, followed by media interviews and family pictures. The rain stopped in time to allow the team to bus to Ohio Stadium for the official team photo and a variety of essential group shots.

Saturday, August 12

The first day in pads produced a number of pad-popping hits, the kind you can hear on the other side of the practice field, including a couple from true freshman Tyler Moeller at linebacker. "He is going to be a good one down the road," predicted defensive coordinator Jim Heacock. "I like his intensity."

Saturday, August 19

The Ohio State defense got to keep the scarlet jerseys thanks to a 66–65 win in the jersey scrimmage. With the score tied at 65, Tressel put the ball on the 3-yard line at the south end of the stadium. A score would have given the offense the win; a stop would crown the defense. Safety Brandon Mitchell knocked down a slant pass from Smith to Ginn Jr. to give the defense its one-point victory.

Monday, August 21

The Buckeyes held a night practice in Ohio Stadium to help prepare for their upcoming prime-time games at Texas and at Iowa. More than 28,000 fans showed up for the practice and autograph session that followed. The Ohio State Marching Band showed up unexpectedly. The crowd loved it. How many other schools could get 28,000 fans for a practice?

4

The Journey Begins

After three weeks of fall camp, the Ohio State players are anxious to hit someone other than their own teammates. The coaches, head coach Jim Tressel included, are equally anxious to see their product perform on the field. And the fans are ready for the top-ranked Buckeyes to begin their quest for the national championship.

Northern Illinois drew the short straw as the Buckeyes' opening-game opponent. The Huskies, under the direction of Joe Novak, are a veteran team that averaged 32.4 points and 444.1 yards per game in 2005. Among their returnees is tailback Garrett Wolfe, a preseason All-American and the nation's leading returning rusher. In games against Michigan and Northwestern last year, the diminutive Wolfe amassed 393 yards rushing and scored four touchdowns.

Nor are the Huskies likely to be intimidated by playing in front of 105,000 scarlet-and-gray-clad fans in Ohio Stadium. They are accustomed to playing teams from the major conferences—in 2003, they knocked off Iowa State,

Alabama, and Maryland—all on the road—on their way to a 10–2 record.

Sure, Ohio State is number one in all the polls. But Northern has been there before.

Tuesday, August 29

Tressel's first weekly press conference draws a large crowd. In recent years those luncheons have been held at the Woody Hayes Athletics Center. But the facility is undergoing a multimillion-dollar renovation that won't be completed until late spring, so this year's luncheons have been moved to the Jack Nicklaus Museum, just a stone's throw from the WHAC.

Asked to assess his team heading into the opener, Tressel replied, "In order for us to be a great team, our seniors will need to have a great year. We have a veteran group of seniors who in my opinion can be great leaders."

Wednesday, August 30

Each week, two of Tressel's assistant coaches meet with the media to discuss the upcoming opponent. First up: offensive coordinator Jim Bollman and his defensive counterpart Jim Heacock.

"I have never been around a team with so many guys capable of making big plays," said Bollman. "And the offensive line is the deepest it has been in my six years here."

From the normally tight-lipped Bollman, that was hearty praise indeed.

Heacock also made an interesting observation: "We have a lot of holes to fill, but one thing that has impressed me about this bunch right from the start is the great effort they give. As a coach, that makes you feel good."

Thursday, August 31

Tressel tells Terry Bowden and Jack Arute in a national radio interview, "In reality, we are probably not as good on offense or as bad on defense as everyone thinks."

Friday, September 1

Tressel, Bollman, and Heacock met with this week's ABC announcers—Mark Jones, David Norrie, and Stacey Dales—to preview the game.

Saturday, September 2

Because of television, kickoff was slated for 3:30 PM in Ohio Stadium. Probably a good thing because it rained last night and the field was covered. The late kickoff gave the field a little time to air out.

Once the Buckeyes took the field, however, they gave Northern Illinois no time to get ready. With quarterback Troy Smith seemingly in midseason form, OSU scored on its first four possessions to jump out to a 28–0 lead.

Smith capped off the first three drives with touchdown passes—the first two to Ted Ginn Jr. and the third to Anthony Gonzalez. Freshman Chris Wells kept the offense rolling on an eight-yard run early in the second period, and the Buckeyes led 28–3 at the half.

The halftime statistics told the story. Ohio State had 297 yards in total offense; Northern Illinois had 179. Smith hit 13 of his 17 passes for 208 yards and the three scores, while tailback Antonio Pittman rushed for 69 yards on 11 carries, 10 more yards than the Huskies' Wolfe.

The Buckeyes' young and inexperienced defense missed a few tackles, perhaps due to nervousness more than anything else, but recorded an interception and allowed NIU to convert just one of seven third-down situations. And they did not give up a touchdown in the first half. That has to be a confidence builder.

Northern Illinois tallied another field goal in the third quarter, but Pittman's one-yard run at the start of the fourth increased the OSU lead to 35–6.

The Huskies' lone touchdown of the day came on a four-yard pass from Phil Horvath to Wolfe with 10:27 to play. The try for two was no good and the Buckeyes wound up with a convincing 35–12 victory.

Smith completed 18 of 25 passes for 297 yards. Ginn had four receptions for 123 yards and Gonzalez four for 53. Pittman topped the 100-yard mark with 111 on 19 carries. The Buckeyes finished with 488 yards of total offense.

Wolfe was every bit as good as advertised, rushing for 171 yards on 26 carries for the Huskies.

There was still plenty of room for improvement on both sides of the ball, but the Buckeyes passed their first test. Now, it's on to Austin and the game everyone has been talking about since last January.

Sunday, September 3

Coming up on Saturday is the game that Ohio State fans have been waiting for: an opportunity to repay the Texas Longhorns for their 25–22 upset of the Buckeyes last year in Columbus.

Texas went on to win the 2005 national championship, posting a 13–0 record and defeating Southern Cal, 41–38, in the title game at the Rose Bowl. The Buckeyes finished 10–2 and a very solid number four in the final polls. But most experts agreed, at the end of the year, Texas and Ohio State were the two best teams in college football.

Texas returns 14 starters, seven on each side of the ball. But the Longhorns are minus All-American quarterback Vince Young, who all but single-handedly upended USC in the championship game. Much to the chagrin of Texas coach Mack Brown, the multitalented Young chose to forgo his senior year and enter the NFL draft. But even without Young, the number two Longhorns opened the 2006 season with a 56–7 thrashing of North Texas to extend their winning streak to an impressive 21 straight. They also have won 18 of their last 19 games at Darrell K. Royal–Texas Memorial Stadium and have scored 40 or more in 12 consecutive regular-season games.

The Buckeyes' young defense is going to have its hands full. Hopefully, the OSU offense, with its vast arsenal of weaponry, will be the difference.

This will be the earliest regular-season meeting ever between a number one and number two team. History is on Ohio State's side. The Buckeyes are 2–0 all-time in such games, defeating number one USC in the 1969 Rose Bowl and number one Miami in the 2003 Tostitos Fiesta Bowl.

Not that this game needs any more hype, but just for good measure it is being televised in prime time by ABC, and *College GameDay* will be in the house to help rev up the excitement.

The Buckeyes have been allotted 4,000 tickets. They easily could sell 10 times as many. Any Texas fan with tickets in hand, and without a real passion to see the Longhorns play, could make out quite handsomely.

Monday, September 4

The Buckeyes held their first practice in preparation for the Longhorns. Getting the players' attention was not a problem.

Tuesday, September 5

A large turnout of national media crowded into the Nicklaus Museum for Tressel's luncheon. They wanted to know the similarities between Young and Smith.

"What separates Troy from some of the other quarterbacks I have been around is his command on the field. The players know he is in charge and is going to make a play when we need it," said Tressel of his senior leader. "Vince Young had that same ability."

Thursday, September 7

The ABC crew of Brent Musburger, Bob Davie, and Lisa Salters arrived in Austin. The fourth member of their team, OSU alum Kirk Herbstreit, along with most of the national media, will get to town Friday for the much-ballyhooed showdown between the top-ranked Buckeyes and the second-rated Longhorns.

Friday, September 8

Musburger graciously took time out of his tightly scripted schedule to meet with a group of Ohio State supporters for breakfast at the team hotel. During his 20-minute presentation, he tossed in a nice little anecdote about Troy Smith, who attended a summer camp sponsored by EA Sports and was a favorite of many of the younger campers because of the time he took with each of them.

"As a young man, Troy made a very favorable impression," said Musburger. "That tells you a little bit about the Ohio State program under the direction of Jim Tressel."

The team landed in Austin early this afternoon. After getting checked in and eating the traditional Friday night meal, which always includes pecan rolls from the OSU Golf Course (a tradition that dates back to Woody Hayes), they headed off to Memorial Stadium for a walk-through.

Usually the latter session involves a brief look-see, after which the team hops back on the buses and returns to the hotel. This one took a bit longer as Tressel allowed his players to familiarize themselves with the stadium, the field, and the lights. He also wanted them to get used to the heat. Temperatures in Austin have hovered in the 100s for the past few weeks, and while the players have been continually hydrating themselves since the first day of fall camp, there really is no substitute for experiencing the real thing.

Saturday, September 9

Saturdays on the road always drag out, especially when it is a night game. The coaches keep the players occupied with unit meetings and individual film study leading up to the pregame meal, which is always four hours before the game. The players also have time to watch other games that might be on and spend some time with their families.

The lobby is alive with Buckeyes fans and expectations. There is scarlet and gray everywhere. It is hard to believe there is anyone left in Columbus.

The team left for the stadium just after 4:30 PM. The police escort helped the buses wind their way through the crowded streets and parking lots. On the way in, they passed the *GameDay* set, where earlier in the day Lee Corso donned a 10-gallon hat, signifying that he was picking the Longhorns over the Buckeyes.

As it turned out, the temperature at game time was bearable, especially once the sun went down. The atmosphere was electric and there were celebrities everywhere: LeBron James and Eddie George paced the Ohio State sideline and Matthew McConaughey, a native Texan, cheered for the Longhorns from a private suite.

Once the game started, the two teams traded punches like a couple of heavyweight contenders, each looking for the other's underbelly. But both missed early scoring chances. Ohio State took the opening kickoff and moved from its own 20-yard line to the Texas 11, but missed a 28-yard field-goal attempt. On the second play of that drive, Smith hit Ted Ginn Jr. on a crossing route and 46 yards later the Buckeyes had the ball on the Texas 31. Ginn was not much of a factor in last year's game, but that would not be the case this time around.

Texas punted on its first possession, but after forcing an Ohio State punt, the Longhorns took over at their own 20 and moved down the field behind the running of Jamaal Charles and Selvin Young, two talented backs with speed and the ability to make tacklers miss. After a pass interference call, Texas was knocking on the door at the OSU 7. That's when sophomore linebacker James Laurinaitis stripped the ball from Texas receiver Billy Pittman, and cornerback Donald Washington scooped it up at the 2 and returned it 48 yards to midfield. The Buckeyes' young defense had stepped up.

Going into the game Tressel had planned to make a lot of substitutions. He had two reasons for that. First, he wanted to see how his young players would do against quality competition. Second, he wanted to keep his men fresh in the Texas heat.

Part of that substitution plan involved playing the second-team offensive line on the third series of the game. So after Washington's return, out trotted center Tyler Whaley, guards Kyle Mitchum and Ben Person, and tackles John Skinner and Tim Schafer. With that unlikely fivesome leading the way, the Buckeyes marched smartly down the field and took a 7–0 lead on a 14-yard pass from Smith to Anthony Gonzalez. The 50-yard drive took just five plays. Gonzalez, who would become one of the major stories of the night, had three receptions on the drive, including a 26-yarder on the first play that put the Longhorns on their heels.

Texas tied the score 7–7 with 1:55 to go in the half on a two-yard pass from McCoy to Pittman. It was the longest drive of the night by either team, covering 78 yards in 13 plays.

The Buckeyes then ran their two-minute drill to perfection as Smith hit four consecutive passes to move the ball from the OSU 34 to the Texas 29 with 22 seconds remaining in the half. Gonzalez had caught two of those passes and had seven receptions for 122 yards—and there was still a half to play. The Longhorns had been concentrating on stopping Ginn. In the process they forgot about the other half of the Buckeyes' talented receiving tandem.

Ohio State took a timeout to set up a play. When the Buckeyes broke the huddle, Ginn, on the left side, had single coverage. The crowd saw it and began to buzz. Smith and Ginn also recognized it and made eye contact.

Ginn was two steps, and then some, past his lone defender when the perfectly thrown spiral landed softly in his hands. The Buckeyes led 14–7 with 16 seconds to play in the half. The Texas crowd stared at the gigantic scoreboard in disbelief.

By halftime, Smith had completed 13 of 19 passes for 219 yards and the two touchdowns, and the Buckeyes had rolled up 258 yards in total offense. The OSU defense had given up 191 yards, but only one touchdown, and had come up with a key turnover.

Sophomore punter A.J. Trapasso kept the Longhorns pinned deep in their own territory with punts of 59, 56, and

Always a popular figure among the Buckeyes faithful, coach Jim Tressel greets fans after his team beat Texas 24–7.

41 yards. But Texas would get the ball to open the second half and the Longhorns were just a play away from tying the score. The OSU defense would have to sustain.

Texas ran the ball two straight times and picked up the first down. On the next play, McCoy threw over the middle, but into the waiting arms of Laurinaitis, who returned the ball 25 yards to the Texas 21. It was the first career interception for Laurinaitis. The Texas defense forced the Buckeyes to settle for a field goal, but OSU led 17–7 after Aaron Pettrey's 31-yard kick and had a little breathing room. Ohio State led by 10 heading into the fourth quarter and was clearly outplaying the second-ranked Longhorns.

The only other scoring opportunity for Texas came with just over 12 minutes to play, but Greg Johnson's 45-yard field-goal attempt was wide to the right. Ohio State then put the game away with a 10-play, 72-yard drive that culminated in a two yard run by hard-charging tailback Antonio Pittman. Pittman carried the ball five times on the drive and also had a reception. Smith completed four of five passes.

Ohio State 28, Texas 7! There would be no more scoring.

Smith certainly did nothing to damage his Heisman Trophy chances, completing 17 of 26 passes for 269 yards and two touchdowns. He was in total command of the game from start to finish, almost surgically dissecting the Texas secondary.

Gonzalez had a career day with eight receptions for 142 yards, and Ginn had five catches for 97. Pittman chipped in with 74 yards on 16 carries. The Buckeyes simply had too much firepower.

Trapasso kept up his stellar play in the second half and wound up averaging 50.8 yards per kick on six punts, the third-best single-game average in OSU history.

The Buckeyes snapped the Longhorns' 21-game winning streak and certainly solidified themselves as the number one team in the nation.

Sunday, September 10

The team got home shortly after 4:00 AM, but no one seemed to mind the late arrival or the bus trip from Rickenbacker Airport to campus.

Monday–Friday, September 11–15

Ohio State has been chosen as the National Team of the Week, while Laurinaitis, who finished the Texas game with 13 tackles, an interception, a tackle-for-loss, and two forced fumbles, was chosen as the Walter Camp, *Sporting News*, and Nagurski National Player of the Week.

Cincinnati is next up for the Buckeyes, who assemble at the Woody Hayes Athletics Center for film study and practice. After the win over Texas, the OSU coaching staff knows it must guard against a letdown.

Tressel has demonstrated a knack for keeping his players focused on the task at hand. In fact, heading into this year, his Ohio State teams owned a combined record of 19–5 the week after playing a ranked team.

And while Ohio State is coming off a convincing road win at number two Texas, the players know better than to over-look their upcoming meeting with the University of Cincinnati on Saturday—not with former Buckeyes assistant coach Mark Dantonio now calling the shots for the Bearcats.

Dantonio was a favorite of the OSU players during his three seasons (2001–03) as the Buckeyes' defensive coordinator.

They respect him immensely as a coach and know he will have his team ready to play when they arrive in Columbus.

Tressel and Dantonio are good friends. They got to know one another in 1983 and '84 while on Earle Bruce's staff at Ohio State. At the time, Tressel was coaching the quarterbacks and wide receivers, and Dantonio was serving as a graduate assistant. When Tressel left Ohio State to become the head coach at Youngstown State in 1986, he hired Dantonio on a full-time basis. The two spent five very successful years together at YSU.

Dantonio coached at Kansas and Michigan State after leaving Youngstown. He was defensive coordinator for Michigan State in 1998 when the Spartans upset the number-one-ranked Buckeyes in Ohio Stadium.

This will be Dantonio's second visit to Columbus since leaving the Buckeyes. He brought the Bearcats to Ohio Stadium in 2004 in his first game as a head coach. The Buckeyes won that encounter, owned a commanding 12–2 lead in the series, and have not lost to the Bearcats since 1897. Additionally, OSU has won all seven games played in Columbus. But a quick look at the game films from 2002 will remind anyone who has forgotten that the Buckeyes were fortunate to escape Paul Brown Stadium with a 23–19 win in their national championship year.

Tressel is not about to let his team get a big head, this or any other week. Still, this is the kind of game he does not enjoy. Dantonio and his wife and children are like family to Tressel. To make matters worse, his nephew, Mike Tressel, coaches the Bearcat linebackers and special teams and is the son of Dick Tressel, who coaches the OSU running backs.

Better to get this one over with and get on to Big Ten play.

Saturday, September 16

As Tressel had expected, Cincinnati was not about to roll over in awe of the Buckeyes.

After Ohio State took a 3–0 lead on a 47-yard field goal by Aaron Pettrey, the Bearcats responded with a five-play, 80-yard drive to take a 7–3 lead with 6:36 to play in the first quarter. It was the first time this year that the Buckeyes had trailed.

Bearcats quarterback Dustin Grutza completed all three of his passes on the drive, including a 22-yard scoring strike to Jared Martin. On the play that preceded the touchdown, he eluded the oncoming OSU rush and picked up 23 yards before being run out of bounds.

It was still 7–3 at the end of the first quarter. Imagine what college football fans everywhere were thinking as that score flashed on their televisions.

But Pettrey added a second field goal early in the second quarter to cut the deficit to 7–6, and the Buckeyes took the lead for good with three minutes to play in the half when quarterback Troy Smith and flanker Ted Ginn Jr. hooked up on a 12-yard pass.

Smith hit all six of his passes on the go-ahead drive, including a 33-yard toss to Anthony Gonzalez that put the ball on the Cincinnati 6. After a holding penalty moved the ball back to the 17, tailback Antonio Pittman picked up five yards. On second-and-goal from the 12, Smith found Ginn on a crossing route and OSU was on top 13–7 at the half.

The teams were fairly even statistically at intermission. Ohio State had 173 yards in total offense and Cincinnati 148. The Buckeyes had run 29 plays and had capitalized on their only opportunity in the red zone on the Smith-to-Ginn pass. The Bearcats had run five fewer plays but actually had an ever-so-slight edge in passing yardage and were moving the ball.

Both quarterbacks had performed well. Smith had completed 11 of 15 passes for 117 yards and Grutza was 9 of 11 for 119 yards.

Following the halftime ceremonies, which included the introduction of former OSU All-Americans Ted Provost and Eddie George as members of this year's Ohio State Athletics Hall of Fame class, the Buckeyes, adjustments made—and no one makes those adjustments better than Tressel and his staff—took the field.

The Buckeyes punted on their first possession. On their second, they turned to Pittman, who provided the spark they needed by picking up 13, six, eight, and 11 yards on four consecutive carries as the Buckeyes marched from their own

40 to the UC 22. Two plays later, Smith and Ginn hooked up on their second touchdown of the day, this time from nine yards out. Suddenly Ohio State was in total command.

Pittman was the star of the game, finishing the day with 155 yards on 16 carries, an average of 9.7 yards per attempt. He had 103 of those yards after intermission, including a 48-yard touchdown run. That play extended the Buckeyes' lead to 27–7 with just under 10 minutes remaining. They added 10 more points before time expired for a 37–7 win.

On Pittman's long run, Ginn leveled an unsuspecting Bearcat with a nasty block just before the Buckeyes tailback crossed the goal line.

Ginn and Gonzalez each had five receptions as OSU's four quarterbacks combined to hit 11 different receivers.

Defensive tackle Quinn Pitcock had a career day for the defense, recording a personal-high three sacks and narrowly missing two more. Pitcock, who had one sack all of last year, is fast becoming one of the best defensive linemen in the country.

After the game, Tressel said, "I can't imagine anyone with a pair of better inside players than Quinn Pitcock and David Patterson."

The Buckeyes had nine tackles-for-loss, eight of which were sacks. They also collected three interceptions one each by James Laurinaitis, Malcolm Jenkins, and Anderson

Russell. It was the second interception in as many games for Laurinaitis, the surprising sophomore from Minnesota.

"I think Cincinnati was the best team we have played this year in terms of being ready to play against us," said OSU offensive guard T.J. Downing after the game. "Their front four is very good and they had our receivers pretty well blanketed the first half. They threw some things at us we hadn't seen before, but we knew Coach Dantonio would come up with something to keep us off balance."

Tressel and Dantonio shook hands after the game and headed to their respective locker rooms, secure in the knowledge that the two schools don't meet again until 2012.

Monday–Tuesday, September 18–19

After three weeks of nonconference play, it's time to get down to business. Penn State is coming to Columbus to start the Big Ten season.

In the team meeting room at the Woody Hayes Athletics Center, where the coaches and players spend much of their time in reflective thought, only two team pictures are on the walls: one of the 2002 national championship team and one of the 1984 Big Ten championship team, the last Buckeye squad to win an outright Big Ten title.

"Our goal every year is to win the Big Ten title outright," said quarterback Troy Smith. "Coach Tressel tells us all the time if you want to have your picture up as Big Ten champions, then you need to win it outright."

The Buckeyes have come close in two of Tressel's first five years at Ohio State. They posted a perfect 8–0 record on the way to an unblemished 14–0 mark and the national championship in 2002. But Iowa also finished at 8–0 that year, so the two teams were forced to share the crown.

In 2005, Ohio State and Penn State had identical 7–1 conference records. The Buckeyes lost to the Nittany Lions, 17–10, in a game that went down to the wire in Happy Valley. Penn State dropped a last-second 27–25 decision at Michigan for its only loss of the season.

"If you want to be assured of winning the Big Ten outright, then you better win all your games," said Tressel. "That is our number one goal every year. If you can do that, everything else will take care of itself."

Since that loss to Penn State, the Buckeyes have reeled off 10 consecutive victories, including six straight Big Ten games, and are 3–0 heading into this year's matchup. Penn State is 2–1, losing at Notre Dame in their second game of the season. Like the Buckeyes, Penn State has lost a number of players to graduation, including talented quarterback Michael Robinson, who was the piston that kept the Nittany Lions hitting on all cylinders in 2005.

Judging by his comments after the Cincinnati game, Tressel, as well as his players, is eager to get going in league play.

"We are anxious for the Big Ten to start and I think our play against Cincinnati showed that at times," he said. But the coach also noted, "From here on out it is going to get tougher, so we need to keep getting better as a team."

Wednesday, September 20

The excitement of beginning league play was augmented by the start of classes today. Ohio State is on quarters academically and it can be pretty quiet on campus between sessions, so it was nice for the players to have the students back and involved. The first day of classes is always a little hectic, especially for the freshmen, who all of a sudden are in an entirely different world. But by the end of the week, things have a way of smoothing themselves out.

Saturday, September 23

Even though Penn State had a loss, this was still a game of national magnitude. The Buckeyes had passed their test at Texas; could they handle Penn State? ABC was here to find out, as was *College GameDay*.

To add to the pageantry, everyone in sold-out Ohio Stadium seemed to be clad in scarlet. Penn State had staged a "whiteout" in Beaver Stadium last year, but it was nothing compared to the "red sea" in the Horseshoe.

It was wet and windy at game time. The two teams punched and counterpunched like a couple of heavyweight boxers throughout much of the first half, but neither could land a haymaker.

Penn State finally took a 3–0 lead on the last play of the half when Kevin Kelly converted a 21-yard field-goal attempt. Kelly had missed from 23 yards on the previous play, but Malcolm Jenkins was flagged for running into the kicker and Kelly made the most of his second chance.

The statistics at halftime reflected the less than ideal weather conditions and were downright ugly. The two teams had a combined total of 183 yards in total offense—99 by Ohio State and 84 by Penn State.

The Buckeyes had gone for the jugular early, but Troy Smith's deep pass to Ginn was intercepted at the Penn State 25, ending a streak of 152 consecutive passes without an interception for the Buckeyes' quarterback. That was about as exciting as it got before intermission.

The halftime program included the introduction of Ohio State's Tyson Gentry and Penn State's Adam Taliaferro. Gentry suffered a serious spinal cord injury in the spring and, although still wheelchair-bound, was able to raise his arm and thank the fans for their encouragement and support. Taliaferro, who incurred a similar injury against Ohio State six years ago, is now almost fully recovered. The two have become friends since Gentry's injury.

Ohio State finally got on the scoreboard in the third quarter thanks to a jump-start from tailback Antonio Pittman.

The 5'11" junior was the catalyst on a nine-play, 75-yard drive in which he had a 19-yard run and caught a 17-yard screen pass. The latter moved the ball down to the Penn State 12-yard line, and Pittman bolted over right tackle on the next play to give OSU a 7–3 lead.

The Buckeyes had the lead, but they were anything but comfortable heading into the fourth quarter. That changed in the blink of an eye as Troy Smith again came to the rescue.

On second-and-nine at the Penn State 37, Smith was flushed out of the pocket and rolled to his right. Seeing no one open, he reversed his field and kept the play alive. Few quarterbacks buy time better than Smith. As Smith was improvising at midfield, Brian Robiskie broke free. Smith's pass hit Robiskie in the numbers two yards deep in the end zone and OSU could take a deep breath at 14–3.

After the game, Kirk Barton was asked what he thought about Smith's play. "I was thinking that when he is in New York [for the Heisman Trophy presentation], they're probably going to show that play a few times," said the big right tackle from Massillon.

Penn State didn't get to be Penn State by throwing in the towel, however. On their next possession the Nittany Lions marched down the field to the Ohio State 5-yard line.

On first-and-goal Tony Hunt picked up a yard over right guard. On the next play, he followed his right tackle down to the 1-yard line. BranDon Snow got the call on third down

Tyson Gentry (right), who suffered a spinal cord injury during spring practice, was on hand to support his teammates against Penn State. Here he talks with former Nittany Lion Adam Taliaferro, who sustained a similar injury in 2000.

and was stuffed by James Laurinaitis and Brandon Mitchell. It was fourth-and-one. Penn State coach Joe Paterno didn't hesitate to send in a play. He was going for seven.

As the Nittany Lions prepared to run their play, the roar in Ohio Stadium was deafening. Unable to hear his quarterback, one of the Penn State linemen jumped prematurely. All of a sudden it was fourth-and-six and Paterno, who knew he could not come away empty-handed, settled for a 23-yard field goal by Kelly.

On the heels of their goal-line stand, the Buckeyes recorded interceptions on Penn State's next two possessions and returned both picks for touchdowns. Just like that it was 28–6 and Penn State fans sat in disbelief.

Jenkins recorded the first pick, returning it 61 yards and atoning for running into the kicker just before halftime. Antonio Smith, who plays the corner opposite Jenkins, got the second and took his first career interception back 55 yards to the end zone.

The Buckeyes also had an earlier interception by Laurinaitis, giving them eight on the year, three more than they had all of last year.

Penn State lost its seventh consecutive game to the Buckeyes in Ohio Stadium. In their last three home games against the Nittany Lions, the Buckeyes have scored just three offensive touchdowns, but have scored four times on defense and once on special teams. Penn State has scored a total of 38 points in its last five visits to Columbus.

The Buckeyes have now defeated both teams they lost to in 2005. More importantly, they have started the Big Ten season on the right foot in their quest for an outright title.

Monday, September 25

Both Ohio State and Iowa are 4–0 on the season and 1–0 in the Big Ten. The Buckeyes are number one in the Associated

Press, *USA Today*, and Harris Interactive polls, while the
Hawkeyes hold the number 13 spot in all three. So it stands
to reason that something has to give when the two teams
meet in Iowa City.

History seems to be on the Buckeyes' side. Ohio State
leads the overall series 43–14–3 and even has a 16–6–2
edge in games played in Iowa City. Still, going on the road
is never easy, and it can be particularly unnerving when the
game is played in prime time, as this one will be.

The Kinnick Stadium crowd will be in a state of frenzy
by kickoff. Night games on national TV can do that, and
this will be just the fifth evening soiree in Iowa history. Additionally, in senior quarterback Drew Tate, the still relatively young Ohio State defense will face its most difficult
challenge to date. A fierce competitor, Tate almost single-
handedly defeated the visiting Buckeyes in 2004, engineer-
ing a very one-sided 33–7 victory. Tate remembers that
game. He also remembers last year when the Buckeyes returned the favor with a 31–6 victory of their own in which
he was sacked four times and the Hawkeyes were held to
137 yards of total offense in Columbus.

Tuesday, September 26

At Tressel's Tuesday press luncheon, much of the talk centered on the visitors' pink locker room in Kinnick Stadium,
designed to soothe the savage beast in Iowa's opponents.

"If you are worrying about the color of the locker room, you probably are not focusing on the task at hand," was the coach's observation.

Wednesday, September 27

During a radio interview with Terry Bowden and Jack Arute, Tressel was asked what has impressed him the most about his young defense, which already has nine takeaways on the year and has held its last three opponents to a combined total of 20 points.

"They have done a great job of keeping their poise, even though everything is brand-new to them," he replied. "Much of the credit for that has to go to our two seniors up front, Quinn Pitcock and David Patterson. They have provided tremendous leadership."

Four games into the season, Pitcock and Patterson also are establishing themselves as two of the premier defensive tackles in college football, already combining for 27 tackles, 7.5 tackles-for-loss, and four sacks.

"I haven't seen everyone, but it is hard to imagine a better pair of inside players than David and Quinn," stated Tressel.

Friday, September 29

The Buckeyes flew into Cedar Rapids on Friday afternoon and checked into the Clarion Hotel. Following the evening meal, they boarded the buses for the 25-minute drive to Iowa City and a brief walk-through in the stadium. Not only was the locker room pink in the truest Hayden Fry (the former Iowa coach and the man behind the pink ploy) tradition, so was everything in the room, including the lockers themselves and the bathroom fixtures.

But the Buckeyes, with 17 seniors on the squad, had been here before. They weren't worried about the color. The team ran through a 40-minute rehearsal on the field and then headed back up the interstate to the hotel.

As impressive as Ohio State's win at Texas had been, there are still some doubters. If the Buckeyes can win this one, on the road, at night, and against a veteran quarterback, they are for real.

Saturday, September 30

The Iowa students were calling for a "gold rush," and the Buckeyes were greeted by a horde of gold-shirted Hawkeyes fans when they arrived at the stadium today. Chants of "Oh-ver Rated" emanated from a handful of students near the *GameDay* set. But the team seemed unfazed by it all.

Sometimes a game just does not live up to its hype. That turned out to be the case on this night. In all candor, the Buckeyes were just too good for the Hawkeyes—on both sides of the ball.

The Buckeyes made big plays on offense and even bigger plays on defense. Add an exclamation point to the earlier win over Texas. Tressel's team played its best game of the year against the Hawkeyes. The final score was 38–17.

Smith was once again the catalyst on offense, completing 16 of 25 passes for 186 yards and a career-high four touchdowns. Tailback Antonio Pittman added 117 yards on the ground in a superbly balanced attack.

Two of Smith's touchdown passes went to wide receiver Anthony Gonzalez. The first one covered 12 yards and gave OSU a 7–0 lead on its first possession. After a four-yard touchdown run by Pittman at the start of the second quarter, Smith connected with Roy Hall just before halftime to give the Buckeyes a 21–10 lead.

When Smith and Gonzalez hooked up on a 30-yard scoring strike on OSU's first possession of the second half, the Buckeyes had an 18-point advantage at 28–10. Smith's fourth and final touchdown pass came with 4:23 to play and closed out the scoring for both teams. It was a great throw by Smith in the face of pressure, and maybe an even better catch by Brian Robiskie, who laid out in the back of the end zone to make the reception.

Iowa did score two touchdowns against the Buckeyes, including the first rushing touchdown of the season by an Ohio State opponent. But Tate, under pressure all game long, could never get rolling. He finished the night completing 19 of 41 passes for 249 yards, including a four-yard touchdown throw at the start of the fourth quarter, but was intercepted three times.

Ohio State finished with 400 yards and had the ball for more than 40 minutes. Iowa finished with 336 yards and had four turnovers.

Cornerback Antonio Smith led the Buckeyes in tackles with six; safety Brandon Mitchell, whose second-quarter interception led to the Buckeyes' second touchdown, had five stops and recovered a fumble. But it was a total defensive effort as the front four applied constant pressure and the linebackers made play after play after play, including fourth-quarter interceptions by James Laurinaitis and Marcus Freeman to snuff out any hope of an Iowa comeback. Defensive end Vern Gholston, one of the most pleasant surprises of the season, added a pair of tackles-for-loss.

The Hawkeyes had been 0–7 when playing a number-one-ranked team. Now they were 0–8.

The Buckeyes are 5–0 and have survived a brutal September schedule.

5

Eyes on the Prize

In their past seven games, all victories, the Buckeyes have defeated five of the most storied programs in college football: Michigan, Notre Dame, Texas, Penn State, and Iowa. Additionally, with TCU losing last week, Ohio State now owns the nation's longest winning streak at 12 consecutive victories.

All of which will mean absolutely nothing if Bowling Green leaves town Saturday with an upset of the top-ranked Buckeyes.

"No one walked out of Iowa City saying, 'Hey, we've arrived,'" said Coach Tressel at his weekly press luncheon. "I think all of our players know that as a team we can get better in every area.

"We are pleased to be 5–0. Our challenge now is to see how we handle success."

Up until the Iowa game, the Buckeyes had, for the most part, avoided serious injuries. Besides Gentry in the spring,

57

the one setback had been senior linebacker Mike D'Andrea. D'Andrea played in 13 of the Buckeyes' 14 games as a true freshman in 2002 and was ticketed for greatness. But first a shoulder injury and then a knee injury took their tolls and he wound up playing in just 17 games the next three years.

D'Andrea hoped desperately to make a comeback in 2006, but it just was not in the cards. The week of the season opener, Tressel announced that his onetime prized recruit would undergo another knee surgery that would end his college career. D'Andrea would work as a student coach in 2006.

The Buckeyes' first in-season injury came in Iowa City. Redshirt freshman Anderson Russell, who had worked his way into the starting lineup at free safety, suffered a knee injury in the first half of the game against the Hawkeyes. A torn ACL will require surgery and he'll miss the remainder of the season. Russell had been playing well. His loss will hurt.

With Russell out of the lineup, sophomore Jamario O'Neal has received a battlefield commission. O'Neal, yet another member of the Glenville High School Alumni Club, lettered as a true freshman, but the vast majority of his playing time has come with the special teams. Now, when the Falcons come to town, he will make his first college start.

Thursday, October 5

Freshman split end Ray Small told Smith he will score against Bowling Green if Smith gets him the ball.

As they had done in three of their first five games, the Buckeyes came out with guns blazing and scored on their first drive.

Troy Smith capped off an assertive nine-play, 64-yard drive with a three-yard touchdown pass to tight end Rory Nicol. It was Nicol's first touchdown reception of the year and just the second of his career. Nicol lettered as a freshman in 2004, but he sat out the 2005 season with a lingering foot injury. His six-pointer against the Falcons was just what the doctor ordered in terms of a confidence boost.

Bowling Green responded with an impressive opening drive of its own, marching from the Falcons' 18 to the Ohio State 33. But on third-and-nine, quarterback Anthony Turner misfired and coach Greg Brandon sent in the field-goal unit for a 50-yard attempt.

Freshman Kurt Coleman blocked the kick and deflected it into the hands of James Laurinaitis, who returned it 14 yards to the Ohio State 47. Laurinaitis already has four interceptions on the year and is quickly developing a reputation for being in the right place at the right time.

Nine plays later the Buckeyes had a 14–0 lead. Tailback Antonio Pittman capped off the drive with an eight-yard run around left end, extending his streak of games with a rushing touchdown to 11.

Pittman added his second touchdown of the day midway through the second quarter after defensive end Vernon

Gholston intercepted a Turner pass and returned it eight yards to the Falcons' 21-yard line. A holding penalty negated a three-yard run by Pittman and moved the ball back to the 31, but Smith hit Ted Ginn Jr. for a 10-yard gain and Roy Hall for 13 more to give the Buckeyes a first-and-goal on the 8. Pittman took it from there and had his first multiple-touchdown game of the year.

Smith, who began the game by completing his first eight passes, was 12 of 14 at halftime. Eight of those had gone to Ginn, who was within one of his single-game career high, set last year at Michigan.

Bowling Green got on the scoreboard in the third quarter with a 15-play, 85-yard drive. Turner hit Corey Partridge from 12 yards out for the score.

The Falcons' scoring drive ate up 8:39 on the clock. The Buckeyes' first possession of the second half started with 6:21 to play in the third quarter. Smith capped off that possession 14 plays later with an 11-yard pass to Small, who caught the ball in the flat and then darted into the end zone for his first collegiate score. His prediction had come true.

Smith then completed his day's work with a 57-yard scoring strike to Ginn to make the final score 35–7 Buckeyes. Smith had three touchdown passes on the day and seven in his last two games. Ginn had a career-high 10 receptions for 122 yards. The 57-yard completion marked the eighth play of 50 or more yards from Smith to Ginn over the past two and a half seasons.

The Buckeyes finished with 387 yards compared to 339 for the Falcons, who actually outrushed OSU. Laurinaitis and cornerback Malcolm Jenkins each had nine tackles to pace the Buckeyes, who for the fourth time in six games had held their opponent to seven points or fewer.

"It wasn't our best effort, but the bottom line is it was a win and we can learn from it," said Tressel. "From now on it is all Big Ten. Everyone in the league either has a loss or has to come through us. We control our own destiny."

Monday, October 9

Michigan State has driven a stake into the heart of Ohio State's national championship hopes on more than one occasion. Most recently, the 1998 Spartans pulled the rug out from under the top-ranked Buckeyes with a stunning 28–24 victory in Ohio Stadium. The Spartans, who were 4–4 coming into the game, rallied from a 24–9 deficit midway through the third quarter. Ohio State would go on to post an 11–1 record and finish third in the final polls, but the sting of that loss is still felt today by the likes of Joe Germaine, David Boston, Michael Wiley, Ahmed Plummer, Andy Katzenmoyer, and Antoine Winfield, just to name a few. Their chance at immortality was gone as quickly as you can say "Go Green."

In 1974, the Buckeyes were ranked number one and had rolled over their first eight opponents by an average of 36 points a game. But on the road against the unranked Spartans,

Levi Jackson's 88-yard run (probably the most famous play in MSU football history) gave Michigan State a 16–13 lead with 3:17 remaining. Back came the Buckeyes, marching down the field as the clock ticked off precious seconds. On first down at the MSU 11-yard line, All-American tailback Archie Griffin picked up five. On the next play, Cornelius Greene handed the ball to fullback Champ Henson, who bullied his way down close to the goal line. It appeared from the press box that Henson had gotten in, but the officials spotted the ball just short of the stripe. The clock was running as the Buckeyes attempted to huddle and run one final play. On the center snap, the ball bounced away from Greene, but was picked up by wingback Brian Baschnagel, who darted into the end zone for what would have been the winning score. As one official signaled touchdown, two others indicated time had expired. With that, the officials ran to the locker room and even though it took 46 minutes to receive an official ruling from Big Ten commissioner Wayne Duke, the game was over.

In 1972, Michigan State fans celebrated by tearing down the goal posts after the Spartans upended the Buckeyes, 19–12, in East Lansing. The decidedly underdog Spartans had dedicated the game to veteran coach Duffy Daugherty, who earlier in the week had announced his retirement. The loss ended the Buckeyes' seven-game winning streak and knocked them from the unbeaten ranks. Griffin fumbled twice in the game, which didn't sit particularly well with Buckeyes coach Woody Hayes. As a matter of fact, the following week at Northwestern, Henson would set a school record with 44 carries, while Archie had just two. Woody had a way of making his point. The loss to the 4–4 Spartans was the only loss of the regular season for the Buckeyes, who went on to share the Big Ten title and played in the first of four consecutive Rose Bowls.

Those three examples indicate why no one on the 2006 Buckeyes team is taking Michigan State for granted. Even though the 3–3 Spartans have lost three in a row, they have talented players, and a win over Ohio State would make their season.

The leader of the Michigan State attack is quarterback Drew Stanton. He and Buckeyes signal-caller Troy Smith got to know each other over the summer at an EA Sports Camp and have continued their friendship into the season.

Tuesday, October 10

At his weekly press gathering, Tressel was asked to compare Stanton and Smith. "They are both competitors and they are both tough, and you know how I feel about toughness in a quarterback. It is the most important thing," he replied.

Cocaptain David Patterson had arthroscopic knee surgery and will miss the Michigan State game for sure, and probably the Indiana contest next week.

Wednesday, October 11

Tressel and coordinators Jim Bollman and Jim Heacock spent an hour on a teleconference call with ABC announcers Brad Nessler, Bob Griese, and Bonnie Bernstein.

"Given the way Michigan State has played the last three games [consecutive losses], what do you say to your team about them?" asked Griese.

"Fortunately, we have played them the past three years and the players on this team know Michigan State could have won all three of those games," was the coach's reply. "We tell them it is Michigan State."

Tressel received encouraging news from assistant coach Darrell Hazell. Tyson Gentry was able to move his toes, hopefully a sign of even better things to come. Hazell was all smiles as he stuck his head around the corner to tell his boss the good news. This game is important—many people see it as the last real test before the season finale against Michigan on November 18—but for the time being all of Tressel's thoughts are focused on one of his players. That is the kind of guy Jim Tressel is.

Two tornadoes touched down in Columbus. High winds and golf ball–size hail pelted the Woody Hayes complex.

Thursday, October 12

The severe weather has passed, but it is still unusually cold and very windy. As Tressel prepared to meet with the media, he told Hazell, "I have never seen anyone who can throw the ball in the wind the way Troy can. His passes just don't change. It's amazing."

Friday, October 13

Upon arrival in East Lansing, the team went immediately to Spartan Stadium. As Tressel took time to go over some last-minute details in the locker room, he had the absolute undivided attention of every player.

This team is focused. There will be no upset if these players have their way.

Saturday, October 14

Early in the week, the forecast for Saturday had been for possible showers. Instead it turned out to be a beautiful, although slightly chilly, fall afternoon with no sign of precipitation.

Michigan State won the coin toss and deferred, electing to kick. Given the Buckeyes' explosive offense, that choice might seem somewhat baffling, but when freshman tailback Chris "Beanie" Wells fumbled on OSU's third play from scrimmage, the Spartans had the ball at the Ohio State 31-yard line.

Spartans fans sensed an upset as Ohio State fans muttered, "Not again."

But as the Ohio State players had said so many times during the week, this was not the same team that lost in 1998.

On MSU's first play from scrimmage Stanton hit running back Jehuu Caulcrick, who wove his way down to the OSU 14. But the Spartans were called for holding and the ball came back to the 24. On first-and-three, Caulcrick was dropped for a loss by defensive end Jay Richardson. On the next play, Stanton's pass to Terry Love was incomplete. Now it was third-and-five. Stanton again dropped back, but before he could get rid of the ball, linebacker James Laurinaitis was in his face. Stanton retreated in an attempt to get away, but Laurinaitis sacked him for a 16-yard loss, taking the Spartans out of field-goal range. The young Ohio State defense had come through again.

Ohio State took over at its own 20 following the Michigan State punt. Smith expertly moved his team down the field, hitting three of four passes, including a 37-yard strike to flanker Ted Ginn Jr. Tailback Antonio Pittman capped off the 12-play drive with a two-yard run behind center Doug Datish and right guard T.J. Downing. The Buckeyes had a 7–0 lead and would never look back.

Pittman's touchdown was his eighth of the year, surpassing his total of seven the previous season, and gave him at least one rushing touchdown in 12 consecutive games. He and Northern Illinois running back Garrett Wolfe had shared the longest streak in the nation, but Wolfe's string came to an end earlier today against Western Michigan.

It was early, but the Spartans were reeling.

At the beginning of the second quarter, Michigan State went for it on fourth-and-two at the Ohio State 36-yard line. Stanton's sneak gained only a yard, however, and the Buckeyes took over at their own 35. Two runs by Wells and a 32-yard completion to Gonzalez moved the ball to the MSU 19. But the MSU defense stiffened and the Buckeyes had to settle for a 32-yard field goal by Aaron Pettrey. It was the start of a 17-point quarter for the Buckeyes, who after punting the ball away on their next possession, forced the Spartans to punt from deep in their own end.

Michigan State coach John L. Smith could either punt it out of bounds or risk punting to Buckeye comet Ted Ginn Jr., which is a little bit like choosing your own poison. He chose to kick to Ginn and the result was lethal. Gathering the ball in at his own 40 and getting a block from Anthony Gonzalez, Ginn split a pair of MSU defenders and then raced 60 yards to the end zone. It was his sixth career punt return for a touchdown, giving him sole possession of the Big Ten record that he had shared with Iowa's Tim Dwight. It also left him two shy of the NCAA record.

Buckeyes fans had been waiting all year for Ginn to break one of the records. The 10,000 or so Ohio State fans who had made the trek from Columbus to East Lansing that day got their wish.

On Michigan State's next possession, Stanton dropped back to pass on first-and-10 at his own 48, but OSU linebacker

Marcus Freeman jumped in front of the intended receiver and picked off his second pass of the year, giving the Buckeyes possession on the MSU 39. It was the Buckeyes' 13th interception of the year and gave them one in each of their first eight games.

After a holding penalty on OSU, Smith and Gonzalez hooked up on a 23-yard completion, taking the ball down to the MSU 26. A nine-yard pass to Ginn and a five-yard run by Smith made it first-and-10 on the 12. But after two straight incomplete passes, the Buckeyes called timeout with 47 seconds remaining.

On the ensuing play Smith was forced to scramble, but somehow he found Gonzalez on a crossing route in the back of the end zone. A perfect pass to his outstretched hands along with the ensuing extra point made it 24–0. Game over!

"Troy put it the only place he could put it if I was going to catch it. It was an amazing throw," said Gonzalez.

Ohio State kicked off to start the second half. The Spartans picked up a first down on their first play from scrimmage on a 10-yard run by Caulcrick. But Stanton was sacked on a third-and-nine by the Buckeyes' Quinn Pitcock and the Spartans were again forced to punt.

As Gonzalez signaled for a fair catch, an MSU player ran into him and was flagged for interference. The Buckeyes took over at their own 47 and five plays later had a

Ted Ginn Jr. and the Buckeyes ran past Michigan State for a
38–7 victory at Spartan Stadium in East Lansing, Michigan.

31–0 lead on a seven-yard pass from Smith to Robiskie. On the play, Smith spun out of one tackle and then broke another before firing a dart to the diving Robiskie. It was a play that almost certainly will appear on *SportsCenter* later tonight.

Ohio State scored again in the fourth period to up the count to 38–0. Michigan State got on the board with just over a minute to play to avoid the shutout.

The Buckeyes rolled up 421 yards against the Spartans, throwing for 239 yards and rushing for 182 more. Smith hit 15 of 22 passes for 234 yards and a pair of touchdowns and also rushed for 10 yards. Gonzalez led all receivers with seven receptions for 118 yards and a score. The seven receptions gave him 34 on the year, six more than he had all of last year.

The OSU defense, meanwhile, limited the Spartans to 198 total yards, including just 63 on the ground. Laurinaitis led the Buckeyes with nine tackles, the sixth time in seven games that he has paced the team, and Pitcock added two more sacks to his résumé, giving him a team-leading seven on the year.

The last-minute (or nearly so) touchdown by the Spartans lowered the Buckeyes' average points allowed to 9.0 points a game, but knocked them out of the national lead.

No matter—the Buckeyes had avoided the upset, in the process becoming just the 20th team in Ohio State history to jump out to a 7–0 start.

Sunday, October 15

Ohio State is number one in the first BCS rankings with a .9731 rating. The Buckeyes are first in the Harris and *USA Today* polls and third in the computer rankings. Southern Cal (first in the computer rankings) is second in the BCS ranking at .9559 and Michigan is third at .9341. Auburn (.7478) and West Virginia (.7375) round out the top five.

"We know the only poll that really counts is the one on January 9," said Tressel.

Monday, October 16

Now that the Buckeyes have gotten by Michigan State, they should have clear sailing until the season finale against Michigan. Ohio State's next three opponents—Indiana, Illinois, and Northwestern, in that order—have a combined record of eight wins and 13 losses. Only the Wolverines on November 18 stand in the way of the Buckeyes' second trip in five years to the national championship game.

Indiana has the best credentials of the three pre-Michigan opponents. Coach Terry Hoeppner's Hoosiers are 4–3 on the year and 2–1 in the Big Ten. They are coming to town with a two-game winning streak after downing Illinois on the road and recording a stunning upset of 13th-ranked Iowa in Bloomington. They had overcome double-digit deficits in three of their four wins, and the victories over Illinois and Iowa represented their first back-to-back Big Ten wins since 2001.

The Hoosiers play with the indomitable spirit of their head coach. Hoeppner, who is in his third year at Indiana after a very successful career at Miami University in Ohio, is both a motivator and a fierce competitor. He demands, and gets, the most out of his players, in the process convincing them that no mountain is too high to climb.

He is also an example of courage. Diagnosed with a brain tumor in the spring, he has since undergone two operations, one of which came after the season started. He also endured the loss of his closest friend, Northwestern head coach Randy Walker, who died unexpectedly of a heart attack in July.

Tuesday, October 17

"Indiana is a lot like their coach," Tressel told the media. "They are tough and courageous. You don't come back from big deficits the way they have unless you have a lot of character. It is fun to watch them on film, because they play with such effort. They are a team on the rise."

They certainly have been so the past two weeks. The win over once-beaten Iowa, whose only previous loss had been to Ohio State, was particularly impressive. It was no fluke; the Hoosiers outplayed the Hawkeyes.

Wednesday, October 18

The game itself took a backseat to an earlier Big Ten announcement that ESPNU would televise the game. It has started to sink in that most Ohio State fans will not be able to see the game unless they have DirecTV. Fans flooded the athletics department with e-mails and phone calls expressing their displeasure and outrage.

Ohio State director of athletics Gene Smith was able to work out an agreement with Tom Griesdorn of WBNS-TV and Chuck Gerber of ESPN that would allow the game to be shown on a delayed basis on both Saturday and Sunday nights. It isn't live, but it's the next best thing.

The other option is to listen to the game on radio. Paul Keels and Jim Lachey, who do the play-by-play and color for WBNS Radio, are two of the best around and many fans routinely turn down the volume on their TV sets to listen to them. But it is one thing to have the option to do so and another to have no choice.

Thursday, October 19

Senior defensive tackle Quinn Pitcock was named as a semifinalist for the Lombardi Award, and sophomore linebacker James Laurinaitis made the cut as semifinalist for the Butkus Award. Both lists will be pared down in late November.

Saturday, October 21

It was a noon kickoff and the crowd for some reason was slow to arrive. Indiana took an early 3–0 lead on a 34-yard field goal by Austin Starr. Tracy Porter's 34-yard punt return had given the Hoosiers prime field position at the Ohio State 15-yard line. But thanks to a couple of dropped passes, IU had to settle for three. Still, they had the lead and it was only the third time all year that the Buckeyes had trailed.

Ohio State punted on its first two possessions as Troy Smith uncharacteristically misfired on his first three pass attempts. Fortunately, that was not to be a harbinger of things to come.

On the Buckeyes' next possession, Smith was again off-target on his first pass. But on second-and-10, he found tail-back Antonio Pittman alone in the flat on a screen pass. Pittman picked up 22 yards and just that quickly the Buckeyes were untracked.

Smith kept things going with a 29-yard run on which he started to roll to his right, then reversed field and raced down the near sideline in front of the Ohio State bench to the Indiana 32. Two plays later, on third-and-one, Smith faked an inside handoff to his running back and calmly lofted the ball into the hands of tight end Rory Nicol, who waltzed untouched into the end zone.

Smith seemingly provides a Heisman Trophy type of play each game. He did so against the Hoosiers on the Buckeyes' next possession. OSU had taken over at their own 47 and in three plays had moved to the Indiana 31. On first down, Smith dropped back to pass, was pressured, pirouetted out of danger, and rolled to his left. There was an open field in front of him, but instead of running the ball, he suddenly pulled up, took a step back, and let the ball go. Somehow, he had seen Ted Ginn Jr. running to daylight. Ginn and the ball became one in the corner of the end zone and Ohio State led 14–3. Smith had provided another Heisman moment.

The Buckeyes' lead ballooned to 21–3 on their next possession as Smith threw his third touchdown of the day, this time a five yard strike to Anthony Gonzalez. Gonzalez also had a 24-yard reception earlier in the drive.

Given Indiana's history of successful comebacks this year, the Buckeyes were not about to sit on their lead when they got the ball back with 51 seconds remaining in the half. Taking over at the Indiana 49, Smith and split end Brian Robiskie hooked up on consecutive completions and, with the aid of a personal foul, the Buckeyes had a first-and-goal at the 1-yard line. Smith then threw a perfect pass to tight end Jake Ballard, who was running a drag route five yards in the end zone, and Ohio State had a 28–3 lead at the half.

The three-play drive had taken all of 31 seconds. It was the first reception of the year for Ballard, a highly regarded true freshman from Springboro, Ohio.

"When a senior quarterback throws the ball to a freshman who hasn't played very much, you better catch it," said Ballard after the game.

At halftime, OSU had 272 yards in total offense, while Indiana had just 65. Hoosiers quarterback Kellen Lewis is going to be a good one, but on this day at least, he was no match for the Buckeyes, whose variety of stunts and blitz packages never allowed him to get into any kind of rhythm.

Halloween is still two weeks away, but the Buckeyes reached into their bag of tricks in the second half as Ginn took the pitch from Smith on an apparent reverse, then delivered a perfect spiral to Nicol, whose defender had been tripped up by the "turf monster." Nicol gathered in the ball and scored his second touchdown of the day and the third by a tight end. The play covered 38 yards and gave Ohio State a 35–3 lead.

"We practice and practice and practice that play and watch duck after duck after duck," joked Smith after the game. "But Ted kept telling us if he got the chance in a game he would throw a spiral, and he did."

While the OSU offense was on its way to a season-high 44 points, the Buckeyes' defense in general, and cornerback Antonio Smith in particular, was keeping plenty of heat on the Hoosiers. Smith was Lewis's worst nightmare, finishing the game with a career-high 12 tackles, including four tackles-for-loss, a sack, and a forced fumble. Eleven of his tackles were solos.

As the team was heading to the locker room after the 44–3 victory, a zealous fan urged the OSU coaching staff to start a Heisman campaign for Antonio Smith.

"Every time I looked up he was making a play," conceded Tressel.

The Buckeyes were 8–0 and 4–0 at the halfway point of the Big Ten season.

Sunday, October 22

Ohio State maintains its hold on the number one spot in the second week of the BCS rankings with a rating of .9764. Michigan moves into the number two spot with a .9451 figure, marking the first time that two teams from the Big Ten have occupied the top two spots. USC slips to third at .9430. West Virginia also moves up a spot to fourth, but trails the Trojans by a wide margin at .7751.

Monday, October 23

Both Smiths, Troy and Antonio, were honored by the Big Ten following their performances against Indiana. Troy, who threw for 220 yards and tied a personal high with his four touchdown passes, was named Co-Offensive Player of the Week. Antonio, the former walk-on, was named the Co-Defensive Player of the Week after his 12-tackle performance.

Tuesday, October 24

Tressel is asked about the possibility of coaching professionally, specifically with the Cleveland Browns if an opening were to occur. "I haven't spent one moment thinking about coaching professionally," he said. "My focus is on this team."

To the coach's way of thinking the matter was closed. Not all the writers felt that way, however, speculating that he had left the door open.

But those people close to Tressel know better. Ohio State is his destination point.

Wednesday, October 25

One of the battle cries of the team during preseason camp was "Get Through September." The Buckeyes did so with a 5–0 record, solidifying their number one ranking with impressive road wins over Texas and Iowa.

Tressel's team has extended that record to 8–0 with three more wins in the month of October and has a solid lead in each of the first two bowl championship series rankings.

To get to 9–0, all the Buckeyes have to do is defeat Minnesota. On paper, anyway, that does not appear to be a problem. The Gophers, riddled by injuries, are 3–5 on the year and 0–4 in the Big Ten.

Still, Minnesota is coached by Glen Mason, and that in itself is cause for concern. "Mace" played for the Buckeyes under Woody Hayes and later returned as an assistant coach at his alma mater between 1978 and 1985. When he left Ohio State to become the head coach at Kent State, he was the Buckeyes' offensive coordinator and regarded as one of the up-and-coming young coaches in college football. From

Kent, Mason went on to Kansas before settling in at Minnesota at the start of the 1997 season.

Mason has always had a soft spot in his heart for Ohio State and was very much in the running to replace John Cooper in 2001 when Tressel got the nod. He will have his team ready to play when it comes to Columbus. This is Homecoming weekend on the OSU campus and one of its alums is coming home.

Additionally, the Minnesota roster is dotted with players from the central Ohio area, all eager to show their families and friends that the Buckeyes had made a mistake not recruiting them. They want their visit to Ohio Stadium to be a memorable one.

And there is one other factor to consider. Tressel's record at Ohio State is a glittering 58–13, including a 34–10 record in Big Ten play, but seven of his 13 losses came in October—and this is Halloween weekend.

Thursday, October 26

Heavy rain moved practice inside.

Saturday, October 28

Winds were gusting up to 35 miles an hour for the 3:30 PM kickoff. Minnesota won the toss and deferred, like most teams, preferring to take the ball in the second half.

Ted Ginn Jr. was deep for the Buckeyes. He had broken his toe while hurrying to a wide receivers meeting the

Wednesday before the Indiana game, but he played against the Hoosiers with no ill effects before news of the injury became public. He also practiced on Thursday before the IU game. But once the news got out, everyone was anxious to see if it would be the same old Ted Ginn out there.

The question was answered in a hurry. Ginn took the opening kickoff at his own 8 and returned it 35 yards to the Ohio State 43-yard line. Apparently, it takes more than a broken toe to slow down the Ginn Express.

The Buckeyes quickly took advantage of their favorable field position, marching 57 yards in eight plays for a 7–0 lead.

Tailback Antonio Pittman, who a week ago saw his string of 12 straight games with at least one rushing touchdown end, carried the ball five times on the drive, including the final 10 yards for the score.

The Buckeyes also scored on their next possession as Aaron Pettrey hooked the ball through the uprights from 42 yards away, despite the whirling winds.

It was 10–0 after two possessions and the Buckeyes didn't seem to be spooked in the slightest.

Then, just for a minute, the Gophers put a hex on the Buckeyes, who fumbled on their next two possessions.

First, freshman tailback Beanie Wells put the ball on the ground at the Minnesota 9. Then, after the OSU defense had forced a punt and the Buckeyes had the ball back, quarterback Troy Smith had the ball stripped as he was trying to avoid a sack. Minnesota recovered at the Ohio State 38. Again the defense held, this time stopping Amir Pinnix on fourth-and-one at the OSU 29. The officials didn't even bother to measure.

The offense, somewhat red-faced, high-fived the defense as it came off the field and then went to work with a renewed sense of purpose.

With Smith in total command, the Buckeyes moved downfield to the Minnesota 18. On second-and-eight Smith checked off to Brian Robiskie, who ran a simple go-route and caught his fourth touchdown pass of the season in the corner of the end zone. It was a perfectly thrown pass. If the strong-armed Smith was affected by the wind, he certainly didn't show it.

The Buckeyes were ahead 17–0 at halftime.

The halftime activities featured the introduction of the 1961 team, on hand for its 45th reunion. That team posted an 8–0–1 record and had captured the Big Ten title with a 6–0 mark. The returning players, all a little grayer now, received a warm welcome from the Homecoming crowd of 105,443. But the biggest ovation came moments later when the OSU Marching Band performed their famous "Script Ohio" and OSU alumnus Jack Nicklaus made his way out onto the field as the honorary "I" dotter.

Nicklaus, the former OSU All-American, NCAA champion, and winner of 18 major titles on the PGA tour, became just the fifth non–band member to dot the "I." Bob Hope and Woody Hayes were two of the others in the very exclusive fraternity.

Nicklaus, who had most of his family with him, was obviously honored and made it a point to acknowledge the crowd by waving his ball cap, which was the same style that Woody Hayes had worn as coach of the Buckeyes.

Nicklaus grew up in Upper Arlington, Ohio, and had entertained the idea of playing football. But Woody quickly set him straight on that point, all but ordering him to stick to golf. As it turned out, that was pretty good advice.

Ohio State kicked off to start the second half. Minnesota took over at its own 20, but on third-and-10, Antonio Smith picked off Bryan Cupito's pass and returned it eight yards to the Gophers' 23. Three plays later, Troy Smith scored his first rushing touchdown of the season on a 21-yard run on which his juke left a defender frozen in his tracks at about the 12-yard line. It was one of those highlight plays that would make *SportsCenter* later that night.

"That play just won him the Heisman," declared former OSU coach–turned–radio analyst Earle Bruce.

Pittman made it 30–0 on a 13-yard run on Ohio State's next possession. The Buckeyes had taken over at the Minnesota 41 after an athletic interception by safety Jamario O'Neal. It was O'Neal's first career interception, but the third of the afternoon by the Buckeyes, raising their season total to 18. The PAT attempt was blocked, but the outcome of the game had long since been decided.

Ohio State added a pair of rushing touchdowns in the fourth quarter, giving them five rushing touchdowns on the day. Beanie Wells scored the first on a three-yard run and quarterback Justin Zwick the second on a one-yard sneak. It was the first career rushing touchdown for Zwick, who is a fifth-year senior. OSU was on top 44–0.

The Buckeyes' defense, meanwhile, was making life miserable for the Gophers, holding them to 182 yards of total offense, including just 47 yards rushing on 26 attempts. When the clock hit 0:00, the Buckeyes had their first shutout since a 20–0 blanking of Northwestern in 2003.

Additionally, the defense extended its string of consecutive quarters without allowing a touchdown to eight. In the last four games, OSU had surrendered just 17 points. On the year, seven of their nine opponents have been held to seven points or fewer.

Ohio State has gotten through the month of October unscathed.

Sunday, October 29

Director of athletics Gene Smith met with head coach Jim Tressel and assistant athletics director of facilities Don Patko and decided to replace the turf in Ohio Stadium. With three weeks to go before the Michigan game, they want the best possible playing surface for the all-important showdown in the Shoe.

The current turf is only a little over a month old. It was put in following the Penn State game on September 23, but due to heavy rains and two frosts, it never took root. Patko and his staff are hoping for better weather this time around, and they have three weeks, instead of two, to get ready.

The new BCS rankings have been released, and Ohio State and Michigan remain in the top two spots. West Virginia is third and Florida fourth. USC, which suffered a shocking loss to Oregon State over the weekend, tumbled to eighth.

Tuesday, October 31

ESPN's *College GameDay* crew came to Columbus to do a piece on Troy Smith and his ability to throw under pressure. They set up shop in the players' lounge in the Woody Hayes Athletics Center. In addition to Smith, they interviewed Anthony Gonzalez, Doug Datish, Brian Robiskie, and coach Joe Daniels.

Wednesday, November 1

Smith was announced as a semifinalist for the Unitas Award, one of two national quarterback awards presented annually.

Thursday, November 2

Defensive tackle Quinn Pitcock, who suffered a concussion two weeks ago against Indiana and did not play against Minnesota last week, was given the okay to play at Illinois. Even though he has medical clearance, the coaches will not make a final decision until after warm-ups on Saturday.

Friday, November 3

Through the first nine games of the year, Ohio State is steamrolling over its opposition by an average of 28 points a game. In their last two games, the Buckeyes outscored Indiana and Minnesota by a combined total of 88–3.

Come to think of it, no one has really given Jim Tressel's team much of a tussle in either September or October. The 24–7 victory at Texas in week 2 of the season has been the closest game. Penn State kept it interesting for a while and, to be fair, so did Iowa, but in both cases the Buckeyes pulled away in the third quarter and put the hammer down in the fourth.

But this is the first week in November, and as former Buckeyes coach Earle Bruce used to warn, "It's the pretenders in September and the contenders in November."

The first November hurdle for the Buckeyes is Illinois. The Illini are coached by Ron Zook, a native of Loudonville, Ohio, a Miami University graduate, and a former Ohio State assistant coach under John Cooper between 1988 and 1990.

Zook is now in his second year with the Illini after three years as the head coach at the University of Florida. His first Illinois team finished with a 2–9 record, and this year's squad is 2–7 and has won just one of five Big Ten games. Still, the Illini defeated Michigan State in East Lansing, and they are coming off an ever-so-close 30–24 loss at Wisconsin. Led by quarterback Juice Williams, a true freshman, they built a commanding lead against the Badgers but couldn't hold on down the stretch—a common problem for young teams.

Williams is an undeniable talent. Ohio State recruited him hard. Many observers have compared him favorably to the Buckeyes' own Troy Smith. But Williams, who prepped at Chicago Vocational High School, elected to stay home and play for Zook.

During his three years at Ohio State, Zook developed a reputation as a tireless recruiter. Players loved his infectious enthusiasm. He has been able to recruit players wherever he has coached and Illinois was proving to be no exception. Landing Juice Williams demonstrates that.

"Illinois is an improving team," warned Tressel. "They play hard and they don't quit. We can't go over there thinking this will be easy, because it won't."

The Buckeyes coach was speaking from experience. In 1983, Ohio State dropped a 17–13 decision in Champaign. Two years later, OSU lost again to the host Illini, dropping a 31–28 verdict when head coach Mike White's son, Chris, kicked the winning field goal as time ran out. Tressel was an assistant coach for the Buckeyes on both occasions. In 2002, Tressel's second year as the head coach at Ohio State, the Buckeyes escaped with a 23–16 overtime win in Memorial Stadium en route to a perfect 14–0 record and the national championship.

Saturday, November 4

The game, the 93rd meeting between the two teams, started out the way most of the first nine games have begun. Illinois won the toss and deferred. Ohio State immediately took the ball and marched downfield for a touchdown.

Chris Wells got the Buckeyes on the board with a two-yard run with 8:16 to play in the first quarter, capping off a 14-play, 80-yard drive for the Buckeyes. Troy Smith hit four of five passes on the drive and picked up eight yards on a third-and-nine from the Illinois 10-yard line, paving the way for the touchdown by Wells.

The Buckeyes made it 14–0 early in the second quarter on a one-yard run by Antonio Pittman. The drive started on the short side of the 50 after the Buckeyes' Curtis Terry recovered an Illinois fumble at the Illini 38. Defensive end Lawrence Wilson, who has been coming along in practice of late and had earned more playing time, forced the fumble.

When Ohio State added a 50-yard field goal by Aaron Pettrey just before halftime, it looked like business as usual as the two teams exited the field.

But in the Illinois locker room, where Red Grange and Dick Butkus had become legends, Ron Zook wasn't about to throw in the towel. With 30 minutes to play, he believed his team was still in it. On the other side of the field, Tressel knew the same thing.

Ohio State had 195 yards of total offense in the first half, compared to just 72 for Illinois. And while the Buckeyes struggled to move the ball against a variety of Illinois stunts in the third quarter, neither team scored and Ohio State seemed to be in control in every way.

After all, the Buckeyes' defense had extended its string of scoreless quarters to 10 and had not allowed a touchdown in the last 11 quarters. Members of the Fourth Estate in the press box were hurriedly checking their media guides in an effort to find the last time the Buckeyes had recorded back-to-back shutouts. As it turned out, they wouldn't need that statistic.

With 11:23 to play in the game, Illinois took over at the Ohio State 47-yard line after a 31-yard punt by A.J. Trapasso. Trapasso, another in a long line of outstanding punters that Tressel has pulled out of his hat at Ohio State, had let one slip off the side of his foot, very uncharacteristic of the usually dependable sophomore.

Aided by a short field, the Illini moved to the Ohio State 26 in three plays and then were the beneficiaries of a pass-interference call against the Buckeyes that gave them a first down on the Ohio State 11. Sometimes the guys in the striped shirts get it wrong; they're only human. But they were dead on the money with this call. Cornerback Malcolm Jenkins and safety Brandon Mitchell had run over the intended receiver like a runaway Mack truck. But by doing so they had saved a sure touchdown.

After picking up just one yard on the next three plays, the Illini were forced to settle for a field goal. Jason Reda's 27-yard kick was good and Illinois avoided the shutout.

Buckeyes fans were miffed, but not particularly worried. That soon changed, however.

On the Buckeyes' next possession, Troy Smith was intercepted for the first time in 141 attempts and the orange-clad Illinois student section came to life in anticipation. But momentum can be a funny thing, and when OSU linebacker James Laurinaitis picked off a Tim Brasic pass on the very next play, the ecstasy subsided. Unfortunately, the Buckeyes could not capitalize on the Laurinaitis interception and had to punt, giving Illinois the ball at its own 20 with 3:43 to play.

After Brasic missed his first two passes, Zook, who had yanked Williams in the third quarter, reinserted his star freshman.

"We couldn't get Juice calmed down out there, so we had decided to sit him a while," said Zook at his postgame press conference. "But with the game on the line, I wanted him in there."

Wide receiver Brian Robiskie and Ohio State were nearly tripped up in Champaign against the Illini. The Buckeyes held on for a 17–10 victory.

Williams responded by hitting three straight passes, the first for 24 yards, the second—a flea-flicker—for 15, and the third for 10 more. All of a sudden, the Illini were at the Ohio State 35. But on his next pass attempt, Williams was leveled by Laurinaitis, who came through untouched and was at full speed when he squeezed the last drop of juice out of the Illinois quarterback.

Back came Brasic, whose three consecutive completions moved the ball down to the OSU 3-yard line. On the next play, Rashard Mendenhall took the handoff, veered to his right, and powered his way into the end zone, somehow escaping the clutches of defensive end Jay Richardson. The Buckeyes' lead was down to seven.

It was the first touchdown the Buckeyes had given up in three weeks and it was just the second rushing touchdown of the year by an Ohio State opponent.

It was a seven-point game and everyone knew the onside kick was coming. The ball seemed to bounce either by or through three or four players before Robiskie covered it at the Illinois 47-yard line with 1:40 to play. Robiskie immediately jumped up and handed the ball to the official and then accepted the congratulations of his teammates before heading back out onto the field for what he hoped would be the Buckeyes' final possession.

The Illini still had two timeouts remaining, so the game was far from over. After three Antonio Pittman rushes into the teeth of the Illinois defense used up all but 18 seconds of the clock, Trapasso got a chance to redeem himself. He responded with a 55-yard punt that long snapper Drew Norman downed on the Illinois 2-yard line with four seconds remaining in the game.

It would take a miracle now. In desperation, Zook tried a gadget play, but the Illinois receiver stepped out of bounds at his own 8 and the game was over.

Ohio State had been tested for the first time this year and had escaped with a 17–10 victory. Good teams find a way to win close games.

"Illinois played us hard and never quit," said Smith, whose Buckeyes were actually outgained by the Illini. "My hat is off to them; they gave us all we wanted."

The 2006 Buckeyes became just the sixth Ohio State team to start a season 10–0. But getting fatheaded wasn't an option. Northwestern was up next and earlier in the day the Wildcats had upset Iowa, 21–7, in Iowa City.

Sunday, November 5

Ohio State and Michigan stay one-two in the BCS ratings. The Buckeyes received all 63 votes in the coaches' poll and all 65 in the writers' poll. They garnered 113 of 114 first-place votes in the Harris poll. Louisville is third in the BCS, followed by Florida and Texas, in that order.

Monday, November 6

We received word that Antonio Smith is one of 11 semifinalists for the Thorpe Award as the top defensive back in college football.

Tuesday, November 7

Calls from Houston and Orlando, respectively, confirmed that Quinn Pitcock is one of four finalists for the Lombardi Award and that sophomore linebacker James Laurinaitis is one of three finalists for the Butkus Award.

Wednesday, November 8

Troy Smith was named a finalist for the Davey O'Brien Quarterback Award.

ESPN is in town to do a story on Laurinaitis as the son of a famous professional wrestler. His father, Joe Laurinaitis, is known as the "Animal" and is one of the giants in professional wrestling circles.

Saturday, November 11

The Buckeyes made quick work of Northwestern, routing the Wildcats 54–10. It's finally time to start thinking about Michigan.

James Laurinaitis set the tone for OSU when he forced a fumble on the opening possession, and Troy Smith threw four touchdown passes. The 54 points were the most for Ohio State since a 72–0 victory over Pittsburgh on September 21, 1996, and the defense played a major role in lighting up the scoreboard.

The Buckeyes converted four turnovers and a blocked punt into touchdowns en route to a 33–10 halftime lead and their 18th consecutive victory—the nation's longest winning streak.

With the stands colored in Buckeyes red, Ohio State made itself at home and recovered fumbles on Northwestern's first two possessions. After Laurinaitis forced the first fumble, Smith started the ensuing drive with a 28-yard pass to

Anthony Gonzalez that put the ball on the Northwestern 27. Four plays later, Brian Hartline caught the first of his two touchdowns on the day, and Ohio State had a 7–0 lead.

Northwestern, which upset Iowa a week earlier, immediately gave the ball back.

This time, Bacher fumbled away the snap on the second play, and Antonio Smith recovered, giving Ohio State possession at the Northwestern 27. After Pittman ran 14 yards to the 1, he bounced off the line and turned right for the second touchdown. Brandon Mitchell made it 21–0 with 3:38 left in the first quarter when he picked off Bacher in front of the Northwestern sideline and returned it 46 yards.

Two years after a 33–27 overtime loss at Ryan Field—its first to the Wildcats in 33 years—Ohio State led comfortably after the first quarter. Unlike the previous week, when the Buckeyes allowed 10 points in the fourth and hung on to win 17–10 at Illinois, there was no drama. Their only difficulties were getting to Evanston.

Scheduled to leave Columbus at 3:30 PM Friday, they had to wait for another plane to arrive from Miami after a truck backed into the nose of their charter. Bad weather then kept them on the ground until 8:00 PM and forced them to land in Milwaukee instead of O'Hare International Airport. They finally arrived at their hotel at 10:30 that night.

Any travel problems on Friday did not appear to affect the Buckeyes on Saturday. Smith matched a season high with his four touchdown passes and threw for 185 yards while completing 12 of 19 with one interception. Pittman ran for 80 yards and a touchdown on 19 carries, and Chris Wells ran for a season-high 99 yards and a touchdown of his own.

C.J. Bacher was 17 of 28 for 212 yards with a touchdown for the Wildcats but threw two interceptions before being replaced by Mike Kafka midway through the third quarter. Tyrell Sutton carried 12 times for 57 yards and caught seven passes for 75, but Northwestern (3–8, 1–6) couldn't hang on to the ball.

"We moved the ball up and down the field, but a fumble here, a fumble there, an interception here and an interception there—you can't make mistakes like that against the number one team in the country," Herbert said.

Now, it's on to face Michigan in The Game.

The Michigan game has been an annual nightmare for the Buckeyes in the recent past. In 13 seasons under former coach John Cooper, Ohio State was 2–10–1 against the Wolverines and never had a perfect November. But they've had better luck since Jim Tressel took over, winning four of five against the Wolverines, who beat Indiana 34–3 while OSU was dispatching the Wildcats.

If Ohio State was looking ahead during the game today, it was tough to tell. The Buckeyes did a good job staying in the moment, although several players admitted it wasn't easy.

"It was real hard not to look forward," Mitchell said. "Now that it's here, it's a surreal feeling."

"It's the biggest rivalry in college football," Pittman. "And it's been talked about for the last six weeks."

And it will be talked about day and night before the showdown in Columbus—number two Michigan (11–0) versus number one Ohio State (11–0).

"It's what you dream about as a little kid, playing in that game," defensive tackle David Patterson said.

The stakes have never been higher, either, with the winner getting to play in the Bowl Championship title game on January 8 in Glendale, Arizona.

Sunday, November 12

The weekly BCS rankings have been released. Ohio State retains its stranglehold on first place. Michigan is second, USC now third, and Florida fourth. Notre Dame moved up to number five.

Monday, November 13

As has been the custom for the Michigan game in recent years, the weekly press luncheon and all player interviews were held today rather than Tuesday. After today, all players and coaches are off-limits to the media. Well over 100 reporters attend the luncheon and interviews.

Coach Jim Tressel met with the media at the Jack Nicklaus Museum and jumped right into the Michigan game, skipping the customary recap of the previous week's win at Northwestern.

"I haven't spent much time thinking about last week," he says sheepishly.

The player interviews were held on the indoor practice field of the Woody Hayes Athletics Center. Tressel selected 10 players—five offensive and five defensive—to be interviewed. Reporters had 45 minutes with each group. Smith was lost in an army of reporters jockeying for position in order to hear what the soft spoken quarterback had to say. Defensive tackle Quinn Pitcock drew the biggest crowd when the defense took the stage.

Tuesday, November 14

Former Buckeyes quarterback Rex Kern phoned. Old No. 10 called this "the biggest game in Ohio State history" and labeled Smith "the best quarterback ever to play for the Buckeyes." Strong praise from a player of his stature.

Wednesday, November 15

Todd Bell of the American Football Coaches Association called to say that Smith and Pitcock have been selected to the AFCA All-America team, which will be announced after Thanksgiving. Additionally, word came that linebacker James Laurinaitis has been named to a first-team berth on the defensive unit of the Football Writers All-America team. The offensive unit will be announced next week.

Friday, November 17

In a normal year, Michigan Week takes on a life of its own. The coaching staff is more intense, the players more attentive. Fans proudly wear their school colors to work and the idle chitchat around the water cooler and in the lunchroom turns exclusively to The Game. Members of the national media descend on Columbus in droves, eager to cover what most sports fans agree is the "Greatest Rivalry in Sports." Those 105,000 or so fans lucky enough to have a ticket to Ohio Stadium are the envy of football fanatics from coast to coast. For this one week, current events take a backseat to The Event.

All of that occurs in a normal year, and this is anything but! Much to the contrary, this year will be accorded a special place in the history of one of the most storied rivalries in college football.

To begin with, both teams will take perfect 11–0 records into Saturday's game. Both were unbeaten in 1970 and again in 1973, but never before have two Big Ten teams owned spotless 11–0 records.

This also will be the first time the Ohio State–Michigan game has pitted a number one team against a number two team. Over the years, there have been numerous top 10 matchups between the rival schools, but never a one versus two.

And never in the relatively brief history of the Bowl Championship Series have both teams been in the picture for the national championship game. To the winner will go all the spoils.

While meeting with the ABC-TV announcers, Tressel received word that former Michigan coach Bo Schembechler has died of heart failure. A native Ohioan and a former member of Woody Hayes's staff at Ohio State, Schembechler was the winningest coach in Michigan history and was one of the true icons in college football. Tressel issued a statement and the decision was made to have a moment of silence prior to the game tomorrow.

Early this evening the team settled in at the Blackwell Hotel, just a little more than a stone's throw from Ohio Stadium. The game of the year is less than 24 hours away.

6

The Game

ESPN *College GameDay* and ESPN Radio *College GameDay* were set up in their usual locations south of St. John Arena, and by 9:30 AM the crowd of more than 2,500 was in a frenzy, waiting to hear the predictions of Lee Corso and Kirk Herbstreit. If Corso knew what was good for him, the veteran coach turned showman would put on a Brutus head when he made his pick.

More than 1,100 media credentials had been given out for the game, including one to a writer from Tokyo. The list from around the country was equally impressive with the *Los Angeles Times*, the *San Diego Union-Tribune*, the *Austin-American Statesman*, the *Houston Chronicle*, the *San Antonio Express*, the *Dallas Morning News*, the *Arizona Republic*, the *Denver Post*, the *Atlanta Constitution*, the *Miami Herald*, the *St. Louis Post-Dispatch*, the *Chicago Tribune*, the *Washington Post*, *The New York Times*, the *New York Daily News*, the *New York Post*, the *Boston Globe*, the *Kansas City Star*, *ESPN The Magazine*, and *USA Today* all in attendance, along with HBO and a number of prominent dot-com entities. Representatives from the BCS and the Fiesta, Sugar, Orange, and Rose Bowls were also on hand. It is hard to imagine a game drawing more attention.

The press box was full and the sidelines were jammed, mostly with media, but also with an occasional celebrity such as Eddie George, Derek Jeter, and the award-winning country-western group Rascal Flatts. If this wasn't the national championship game, it was the next best thing. And for Ohio State fans it was more important anyway.

To them this was about more than extending the Buckeyes' 18-game winning streak or becoming the first team ever to win two one-versus-two showdowns in the same year. This was more important than being rated number one from wire to wire or capturing the school's first outright Big Ten championship since 1984. This was about beating Michigan, and little else mattered.

Over the years, Ohio State has played in a number of big games. Every Michigan game is important. The 1969 Rose Bowl, and subsequent national championship, was huge. The two-game series with Notre Dame in 1995 and '96 focused the national spotlight on the Buckeyes. So did the Texas games the past two years. But in the 116 years since Ohio State first began fielding a football team, this was shaping up as the most important game ever played by the Buckeyes.

Prior to the game, the team walked from the hotel to St. John Arena for the skull session, where more than 13,000 fans gather before each game to hear the Ohio State Marching Band rehearse its pregame and halftime show.

As the team made its way down the southeast ramp and onto the floor there was a deafening roar. Then silence, as first a senior and then the head coach offered a few thoughts. The ovation that Tressel received was extremely moving. This is a man who can do no wrong in the eyes of the Buckeyes faithful.

"This is the day," he said with a raspy voice, the result of a sore throat that had been bothering him the latter part of the week. "Our seniors are the best. Go Bucks!"

As coach Woody Hayes used to say, "All the hay is in the barn" at this point. All that was left to do now was to play the game.

Both teams came into the game with impressive numbers. Ohio State led the Big Ten in scoring offense at 35.8 points a game and led the nation in scoring defense at 7.8 points a game. Michigan led the Big Ten in total defense, giving up just 231.5 yards per game, and was number one in the conference against the run, allowing just 29.9 yards per game.

Ohio State had the home-field advantage and was considered a slight favorite. Most of the experts were predicting a low-scoring game that would go right down to the wire. Well, at least they got the last part of the equation right.

Former Ohio State and NFL standout Paul Warfield was the Buckeyes' honorary captain for the day. He accompanied the team captains to midfield and was given the honor of flipping the coin. Michigan called heads. It came up tails. Game on!

Michigan took a quick 7–0 lead, going 80 yards in seven plays with relative ease on its first possession. Junior quarterback Chad Henne was perfect on four passes, three of which went to wide receiver Mario Manningham, moving his team inside the OSU 1-yard line in six plays. Tailback Mike Hart scored around right end on the next play. The Buckeyes would have to come from behind.

Smith immediately went to work and took his team down the field for the tying touchdown, a one-yard pass to Roy Hall in the right corner of the end zone and almost directly in front of the Michigan cheering section. The Buckeyes converted four third-down plays on the 69-yard drive, including three completions to Hall, one of which was on third-and-16.

The track meet was on.

The Buckeyes took a 14–7 lead early in the second quarter on a 52-yard run by freshman tailback Beanie Wells, who had come in to give starter Antonio Pittman a breather. It was the longest run of the year for Wells, who was hit in the backfield but spun away from the tackler and then burst to daylight through a gaping hole on the right side. The two-play, 58-yard drive took all of 57 seconds.

Running back Chris Wells's 52-yard touchdown run against Michigan sent the Columbus crowd into a frenzy.

The Buckeyes forced Michigan to punt on its next possession and Ted Ginn Jr. called for a fair catch at his own 9-yard line. On second-and-six, Smith made another one of his patented Heisman moves, somehow eluding the oncoming rush and then spinning out of trouble and finding Brian Robiskie for a 39-yard pickup.

Robiskie, the son of Cleveland Browns assistant coach Terry Robiskie, made a nice catch on the sideline, spun out of trouble himself, and almost went the distance before being tripped up just past midfield. After a nine-yard gain by Pittman, Smith faked to Wells on a dive play and then went up top to Ginn, who caught the ball between two defenders. The Buckeyes had gone 91 yards in four plays and led 21–7.

"We hoped we might catch them thinking we were going for the first down," said Tressel.

Michigan responded with an impressive 80-yard march of its own to cut the deficit to 21–14 with 2:28 to play in the second quarter. Hart moved the ball to midfield with a 30-yard run and four plays later Henne and Adrian Arrington hooked up on a 37-yard touchdown on which Arrington slipped two tackles on his way to the end zone.

Michigan appeared to have regained the momentum, but Ohio State had other ideas. Taking over at their own 20-yard line, the Buckeyes executed their two-minute offense to perfection, marching smartly down the field on a nine-play, 80-yard scoring drive. Smith hit eight of nine passes on the drive, the last of those an eight-yard scoring strike to Anthony Gonzalez on a slant.

Ohio State led 28–14 at the half and had 320 yards in total offense. Smith had completed 21 of 26 passes for 241 yards and three touchdowns. His touchdown pass to Gonzalez, who is almost unstoppable on the slant, was his 29th touchdown

pass of the year, tying the school single-season record origi-
nally set by Bobby Hoying in 1995. The Buckeyes also had
rushed for 79 yards on 10 carries against the Wolverines'
stout run defense.

Ohio State would get the ball to start the second half and
a quick score could put the game out of reach. Instead, the
Buckeyes were forced to punt, and Michigan took over on
its own 40.

Just as they had done to open the game, the Wolverines
struck quickly, moving 60 yards in five plays for their third
touchdown of the day, which was one more than any of the
Buckeyes' first 11 opponents had managed.

Hart carried the ball on the last four plays of the drive,
picking up eight, 33, 16, and two yards, the last one for the
score.

All of a sudden it was a seven-point ballgame.

In his previous two starts against Michigan, Smith had
not turned the ball over. That streak came to an end on the
Buckeyes' next possession, when Alan Branch grabbed a
deflected pass at the Ohio State 25-yard line. Smith was
looking for Robiskie on the play, but Robiskie was popped
by a pair of Michigan defenders just as the ball got there
and the ball bounced into the air and into Branch's hands.

But after Hart picked up five yards, he was dropped for a
two-yard loss by Laurinaitis. Henne then misfired on third
down and Michigan had to settle for a 22-yard field goal by

Garrett Rivas. The Wolverines had cut the deficit to 28–24 but had not scored a touchdown. The Buckeyes' defensive stand on that series would turn out to be the difference in the game.

Again, the Buckeyes answered. This time it was Pittman, who burst through a gaping hole on the right side courtesy of Steve Rehring and T.J. Downing and raced 56 yards for his 13th touchdown of the season. This time, the two-play, 65-yard drive took 37 seconds.

"I don't think anyone laid a glove on him," Tressel said afterward during the postgame press conference.

It was 35–24 and the Buckeyes had some breathing room.

But strange things happen in the Ohio State–Michigan game, and just before the end of the third quarter the Wolverines recovered an errant snap from center at the Buckeyes' 25-yard line. Hart's third touchdown made it 35–31 with 14:41 to play in the game.

The Wolverines had scored 10 points off two Ohio State miscues. Coming into the game, the Buckeyes had committed 13 turnovers on the season, but had not given up a single point. The Ohio State offense, meanwhile, had scored 127 points off 27 opponent turnovers.

The Buckeyes then took over at their own 26 and moved the ball to the Michigan 28 before fumbling for the second consecutive series when the center snap hit a divot and dribbled into the OSU backfield, where it was recovered by the

Wolverines' LaMarr Woodley. The normally efficient OSU offense had squandered a key opportunity to widen the lead.

After a Michigan punt, the Buckeyes got the ball back
at their own 17-yard line and this time they were not to be
denied. Smith marched his team toward the south stands
and delivered a 13-yard scoring strike to Robiskie, who just
managed to get his foot down before falling out of bounds.
The play was reviewed but upheld, and the Buckeyes had
a 42–31 lead with 5:38 to play. With that, Smith had his
fourth touchdown pass of the day and undisputed possession of the school single-season record.

Michigan wasn't about to concede. The Buckeyes had
gone 83 yards in 11 plays, and the Wolverines responded by
going 81 yards in 11 plays to cut the lead to 42–37. Henne hit
eight of 11 passes on the drive, the last of them a 16-yard scoring toss to tight end Tyler Ecker. The two-point conversion
made it a three-point ballgame.

The record crowd of 105,708 was on its feet for the ensuing onside kick. Ginn, who had enjoyed a monster day
with eight receptions for 104 yards, fielded the ball at the
Michigan 48 for his most important grab of the day.

A glance at the scoreboard showed 2:16 remaining on
the clock. Michigan was out of timeouts, but the Buckeyes needed a first down to guarantee the Wolverines did
not get the ball back. The always-dependable Pittman
picked up nine yards on the first play. On third-and-two,

Offensive lineman Alex Boone joins in the celebration after Ohio State's 42–39 victory over Michigan.

his six-yard run to the Michigan 34 moved the chains. The Buckeyes would not need to run another play. The game was over.

Ohio State finished with 503 yards in total offense, including 187 yards rushing. Smith threw for 316 yards and rushed for 12 more, giving him 1,051 yards in total offense in his three games against Michigan. Pittman ran for 139 yards and averaged 7.7 yards per carry. The OSU defense was led by Laurinaitis, who collected nine tackles and four sacks. The Ohio State offensive line, it should be noted, surrendered just one sack.

With the win, Smith becomes just the second Ohio State quarterback to lead the Buckeyes to three consecutive wins over the Wolverines. The first, the now-91-year-old Tippy Dye, met Smith on Friday and was in attendance at the game.

At the skull session, Smith told the crowd, "I have been at this university for five years. I came here as a boy. I leave here as a man."

Actually, he leaves here as The Man!

The Buckeyes have won the Big Ten title outright. There will be a new picture hanging in the remodeled Woody Hayes Athletics Center.

Big Ten commissioner Jim Delany presented the Big Ten championship trophy to Coach Tressel and the team in the jubilant OSU locker room. The Buckeyes have put the wraps on a perfect 12–0 season and in the process locked up a spot in the BCS title game in Arizona on January 8.

It will be Ohio State's second appearance in the national championship game in five years. Tressel's Buckeyes won the title following the 2002 season with a double-overtime win over previously unbeaten Miami, snapping the Hurricanes' 33-game winning streak.

It will also be OSU's fourth trip in five years to the Valley of the Sun. In addition to the 2002 championship game, the Buckeyes played in the Tostitos Fiesta Bowl following the 2003 and 2005 seasons. The Phoenix area is becoming a home away from home for the Buckeyes.

Ironically, following last year's 34–20 win over Notre Dame in the Fiesta Bowl, one of the writers asked Troy Smith if the players knew where next year's national championship game would be played.

"We know," said Smith with a smile. "It is right back here and we would love to come back."

Thanks to Smith, whose four touchdown passes against Michigan virtually assure the Ohio State quarterback of becoming the school's seventh Heisman Trophy winner, the Buckeyes are indeed headed back to the desert.

"Today you proved you are the best team in the Big Ten," said Delany. "On January 8 you will prove you are the best team in college football."

Tressel graciously accepted the trophy, then handed it to Smith and his fellow cocaptains, center Doug Datish and defensive tackles Quinn Pitcock and David Patterson.

"This belongs to our seniors," he said as a roar erupted from the players. "I am so proud of you. Remember, we still have one game to go."

The coach and cocaptains then headed to the postgame press conference on the third floor of the southeast tower in Ohio Stadium. The victory bell was ringing above them as the players entered the interview room.

On this day, the interview room, which is always crowded, resembled Times Square on New Year's Eve. All that was missing was Dick Clark and some confetti. Nearly every inch of floor space was occupied by either a camera or a reporter with notebook and tape recorder in hand.

As is the normal procedure, first Tressel and then the players issued opening statements on the game. All were complimentary of Michigan and the effort the Wolverines had given. It had been billed as the game of the year and it certainly was just that.

Following their opening statements, the coach and his four captains took questions.

One of the first came from Rusty Miller, the veteran Associated Press sports editor from Columbus, and was directed to Tressel. "Should the Buckeyes and Wolverines be rematched in the title game?" Miller asked.

Tressel had gotten the same question from ABC sideline reporter Bonnie Bernstein immediately following the game.

"I really haven't had time to think about that. Whoever we play will be a worthy opponent. There is a lot of football left to be played. For the time being, I just want to enjoy this game and congratulate our seniors for winning the outright Big Ten title. That is our number one goal every year," Tressel replied.

7

Waiting for an Opponent

There appear to be four legitimate challengers for Ohio State in the Fiesta Bowl: Michigan, Southern California, Florida, and Arkansas.

Michigan's regular season is over. The Wolverines finished with an 11–1 record, having soundly beaten Notre Dame, and having handed once-beaten Wisconsin its only loss before taking the Buckeyes down to the wire.

Southern Cal still has games with Notre Dame and crosstown rival UCLA. Two wins could conceivably catapult the Trojans ahead of Michigan in the BCS standings and land them in their third championship game in three years.

Either Arkansas or Florida is expected to emerge from the Southeastern Conference. Both are considered long shots.

The Razorbacks were soundly beaten by Southern Cal in the first week of the season, and even though All-American running back Darren McFadden saw only limited action in that game, it seems unlikely that Houston Nutt's once-beaten team will move ahead of USC if the Trojans win out.

Besides, the Razorbacks still have to play LSU before appearing in the SEC championship game.

Florida's case is somewhat stronger. The Gators' only loss was a seven-point loss at Auburn. If they can get by in-state rival Florida State on November 25 and then win the SEC championship game a week later, they will finish at 12–1 and will have made a strong case for themselves. Still, USC will need to stumble, and even then there is no guarantee that the Gators will supplant Michigan at number two.

Some members of the media are favoring a rematch with Michigan, arguing that the Buckeyes and Wolverines are the best two teams in college football. And, if that is the case, there should be a second game between the two Big Ten powerhouses.

Others argue that, as good as Michigan is, there is no need for the two teams to play again. Michigan had its chance and came up short. Give someone else a shot at the Buckeyes. What would a rematch prove, anyway, especially if the Wolverines won? Wouldn't it be better to have Ohio State play a conference champion instead of a team that finished second in its own league?

Monday, November 20

The BCS rankings were released yesterday and Ohio State and Michigan held on to the top two spots, respectively.

The Buckeyes had a perfect score. USC was third, Florida fourth, and Notre Dame fifth. Some experts still consider Notre Dame a dark horse contender, but their decisive loss to Michigan earlier in the year make it highly unlikely that they could move around the Wolverines.

All eyes will be on next week's nationally televised show-down between USC and Notre Dame in the Los Angeles Coliseum. If the Trojans win, and do so convincingly, will it be enough to catapult USC over Michigan?

Tuesday–Friday, November 21–24

Thanksgiving week. No practice. Players are encouraged to get in a voluntary lift if they can, but it is voluntary. After 12 weeks of football, the important thing to Tressel is that his players get home and spend time with their families.

The Buckeyes coach, incidentally, is a proponent of the current Big Ten policy of not playing league games after Thanksgiving.

"We bring the players in early and ask a lot of them," he told a writer on Monday. "It is only right that we not ask them to stay here over Thanksgiving, even if that means not having a bye week."

The coach's preference would be for the NCAA to move the start of the season up a week, which would allow for a bye week.

Saturday, November 25

USC upended visiting Notre Dame, 44–24, in the Coliseum, knocking the Irish out of the national championship picture. All that stands between the Trojans and a trip to Arizona is next week's game with cross-town rival UCLA. The Bruins have lost four of their last six games and will be decided underdogs.

Sunday, November 26

Southern Cal moved around Michigan into second place in the BCS standings.

Monday–Wednesday, November 27–29

Players are required to get in two lifts in the weight room.

Thursday, November 30

The team meeting was followed by a film session to review the Michigan game. The players and coaches normally look at the game film a day or two after the game, but due to the excitement surrounding the Michigan game, Thanksgiving, and recruiting, this was the first time the players had seen the film.

Seniors Anthony Gonzalez and Stan White Jr. were named to first-team spots on the CoSIDA Academic All-America team. James Laurinaitis was a second-team pick.

The decision to install artificial turf in Ohio Stadium was announced by Don Patko, associate athletics director for facilities. The Stadium has had a natural grass carpet since 1990.

Friday, December 1

The team held its first bowl practice, a two-hour session in the Woody Hayes Athletics Center.

Saturday, December 2

Hard practice Saturday morning. The Buckeyes still don't know their opponent, but will find out tomorrow. Final exams are next week, so the next practice won't be until Wednesday.

Tressel and the rest of the OSU coaching staff watched the UCLA–Southern Cal and the Florida-Arkansas games from the Ohio Stadium press box while entertaining a group of recruits and their families.

In one of the shockers of the year, UCLA, which had lost seven straight to USC, downed the Trojans, 13–9, eliminating Pete Carroll's team from championship contention.

The Buckeyes will play either Michigan or Florida in the BCS title game. If the Gators falter in the SEC championship game, there will be a rematch between Ohio State and Michigan. If the Gators win, the voters will have to decide on the most worthy opponent.

When Tressel left the Stadium, the game was still going on, but it was apparent that Florida was on its way to the SEC crown. As a voter in the *USA Today* coaches' poll, he was in a bind. No matter how he voted, it was a no-win situation, and ethically it did not seem right to him for Ohio State to vote on which team the Buckeyes should play.

Sunday, December 3

Tressel met with director of athletics Gene Smith to discuss his feelings on not voting. Smith was in complete accord. Later, the university issued a statement saying that Tressel would abstain from voting in the final coaches' poll.

As expected, his action sparked spirited discussion among fans, media, and even a couple of coaches. But Tressel, as he always does, stood up for what he believed to be right.

Shortly after noon, the Buckeyes held their annual Appreciation Banquet. During the three-hour program, each senior gets a chance to talk about his time at Ohio State and then gives a rose to a loved one. Some speeches are humorous, others very touching. The one common thread is the players' deep feelings for one another and the friendships they have made during their time at Ohio State.

The banquet concluded just before 4:00 PM. About an hour later, Gene Smith received word that Ohio State will play Florida. The Gators have moved around Michigan into second place in the final rankings. Florida finished at 0.9445 and Michigan at 0.9345. As it turns out, Tressel's vote would not have made a difference. The voters did not want a rematch.

The Buckeyes, who become the first team in BCS annals to lead the rankings from wire to wire, finished with a final rating of 0.9999.

After the banquet, linebacker James Laurinaitis and graduate assistant coach Doug Phillips flew to Charlotte, North Carolina, for the Bronko Nagurski Award, which honors that organization's National Player of the Year. Laurinaitis is one of four finalists.

Around 7:30 PM Tressel and the captains met with the media to discuss the matchup with the Gators. Tressel did a live interview with Thom Brennaman from Fox Sports, and Troy Smith did a similar piece with ESPN.

Coach and quarterback walked out of the Woody Hayes Athletics Center a little after 9:00 PM. It is time to start preparing for the BCS title game.

At long last, Ohio State has an opponent.

Monday, December 4

Laurinaitis won the Nagurski. He is the first Ohio State player and the first sophomore to win the award. Because he has an exam Tuesday morning, Laurinaitis had to leave the awards banquet in Charlotte before the winner was announced. On the way to the airport, a member of the board told him he had won. Ohio State assistant coach Luke Fickell, who was also at the ceremony, accepted on behalf of his star linebacker.

8

The Long Layoff

While much, make that *most*, of the attention following the November 18 Michigan game has been focused on whom Ohio State would play in the January 8 national championship game, there also is a lot of discussion about the 51-day layoff between games. Whoever the opponent, unless it had been Michigan, would have a much shorter break—and most people consider that to be a definite advantage.

Coach Tressel does not share that view, however. He had heard the same argument in 2002 when the Buckeyes played Miami for the national title. But after a 41-day hiatus, Ohio State upset the top-ranked Hurricanes in double overtime even though Miami had concluded its regular season two weeks after the Buckeyes had played their final game.

Last year, when Ohio State downed Notre Dame, 34–20, in the Fiesta Bowl, the Buckeyes were coming off a 43-day hiatus. Again, Notre Dame had played two games after the Buckeyes had wrapped up regular-season play.

Indeed, Tressel has proven to be a master at making the most of his team's time off prior to a bowl game. His 4–1 record since coming to Ohio State is proof of that. The man has few peers when it comes to calling plays in a big game, and he is absolutely lethal when given extra time to prepare.

Still, 51 days is a long time, and the OSU coaching staff has huddled long and often in an attempt to map out the best strategy for players and coaches alike. This is a recruiting period, so the coaches will be scouring the country talking to the nation's top high school prospects. The Buckeyes are 12–0 and about to play in the national championship game, but Tressel isn't about to take anything for granted when it comes to recruiting, which is anything but an exact science.

Senior defensive tackle Quinn Pitcock and his family flew to Houston for the Lombardi Award ceremony. Pitcock was one of four finalists for the award, which was won last year by the Buckeyes' A.J. Hawk. The other three finalists were LaMarr Woodley of Michigan, Paul Posluszny of Penn State, and Justin Blaylock of Texas. The Buckeyes beat all three teams during the 2006 season.

Joel Penton was named winner of the Wuerffel Trophy, which goes to the college football player who best combines community service with academic and athletic success. Penton talked with Wuerffel by phone. Afterward we joked that his sack in the Michigan game didn't hurt him any.

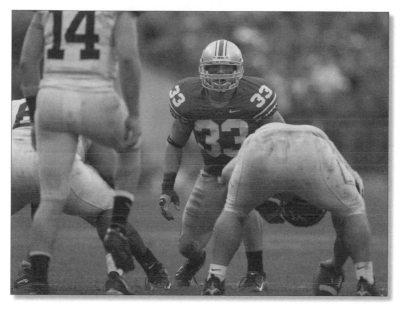

James Laurinaitis was the anchor of a young Buckeyes defense. The sophomore linebacker led the team in tackles and won the Nagurski Award as the nation's best defensive player.

Wednesday, December 6

Smith, Laurinaitis, and I flew to Orlando for the College Football Awards show and were met at the airport by the Orlando police, who escorted us to waiting cars that took us to the hotel. As Laurinaitis was getting out of the police truck, a town car passing on the right struck the door, necessitating an accident report. James was embarrassed, but Smith got a big laugh out of it and needled Laurinaitis about it during the trip to the hotel. After checking in at the Boardwalk Hotel, the players went to the ESPN Club for dinner. Most of the players from the other schools were already there. A couple of former Buckeyes were also on hand, including Outland Trophy and Lombardi Award winner John Hicks, Kirk Herbstreit, and Judd Groza.

Michigan's Woodley is the winner of the Lombardi Award.

Thursday, December 7

The players spent the day relaxing and doing some photo shoots for the Football Writers All-America team.

There was a reception and dinner at the hotel for the three Butkus Award finalists—Laurinaitis, Posluszny, and Patrick Willis of Mississippi. Tressel, who flew in late Wednesday and spent the morning and afternoon recruiting, attended the dinner and then went to the awards show.

The first presentation was the Davey O'Brien Award, which went to Smith. Willis edged out Laurinaitis for the Butkus Award. Ohio State's only winner of the Butkus was Andy Katzenmoyer in 1997. Chris Spielman and A.J. Hawk are two of the more notable Ohio State players who inexplicably did not win it.

9

The Heisman Trophy

Troy Smith and I flew to New York for the Heisman presentation. Pitcock flew to Los Angeles for the Lott Award (the second year in a row that the Buckeyes have had a finalist), and Laurinaitis stayed in Orlando for the taping of the *Cingular/ABC Sports All-America Show*, which recognizes the Football Writers Association of America's team. Smith also was on the Football Writers team, but because of his commitments in New York could not stay for the taping and dinner.

We left Orlando early this morning for New York City, meeting in the lobby of the Boardwalk Disney World hotel at 6:00 AM. We were met by a limo and an ESPN crew at the airport in Newark. As we waited for our luggage, a horde of autograph seekers descended on Troy and Arkansas running back Darren McFadden, who had been on our flight. Even though the players had flown under aliases, the autograph hounds had still managed to sniff them out. It took a New York City police officer to give the two Heisman finalists a little breathing room.

Once we had our luggage, we piled into the limo (nine of us including the ESPN camera crew) and headed into The City. This was the first visit for either Troy or Derek, and TV was there to capture every moment of the ride in.

Before checking in at the hotel, we stopped near the ESPN Zone to get shots of Troy and Derek taking in the sights. But it was so cold and blustery that both players hopped back into the car after a block or so.

Next stop was the Sheraton, where we were met by Rob Whalen and Tim Henning of the Heisman Trust Foundation. Over lunch, they reviewed the agenda for the next two days. Brady Quinn, the third finalist, was not there. He had flown from Orlando to Baltimore to receive the Johnny Unitas Award, which would be presented later in the day. The Notre Dame quarterback was scheduled to come to New York on Saturday.

After lunch, both players checked into their rooms to get some rest. That evening they attended the Wendy's High School Heisman Dinner at the hotel. Troy then headed off with a couple of friends to enjoy the sights and sounds of the Big Apple.

Saturday, December 9

It was a long day, but one that Troy and his family will always remember.

The day officially started with lunch at ESPN Zone. Quinn had flown in earlier in the morning and the three finalists were together for the first time. As they did a series of interviews inside, fans outside pressed their faces against the window in an effort to get a better look at the three young celebrities.

Later, as they rode back to the hotel, the three of them discussed their favorite rappers. There was no consensus winner and I certainly was no help, as Smith pointed out.

Back at the hotel, all three players signed Heisman footballs and then headed to their rooms to get some rest. Troy used the time to make sure his mom, Tracy, and sister, Brittany, had arrived safely from Cleveland.

We boarded the bus for the Nokia Theater about 6:00 PM. Seating for the nationally televised show didn't start until 7:30, but the three principals and their guests needed to be in place well in advance of the actual air time. At the theater, Troy, Derek, and Brady were hustled off to makeup and a quick briefing. The rest of the guests entertained themselves at a reception, which included many of the past Heisman winners.

All interested parties were in their seats shortly after 7:30 PM. Prior to the actual start of the show, emcee Chris Fowler charmingly engaged the audience, giving us a rundown of the format. In little more than 60 minutes, the winner of the 2006 Heisman Trophy would be announced.

The actual announcement caught Smith somewhat off guard. He had expected Fowler to name the winner. Instead, it was Judge John Sprizzo, a trustee of the Heisman Trust, who opened the envelope and ended the suspense:

"The winner of the 2006 Heisman Trophy, from Ohio State University, Troy Smith."

The audience in New York City's Nokia Theater stood and applauded. Former Ohio State Heisman winners Howard "Hopalong" Cassady, Archie Griffin, and Eddie George were there, as was former OSU teammate and current Indianapolis Colts safety Mike Doss.

Smith accepted congratulations from Quinn and McFadden, neither of whom appeared surprised at Smith's selection. Then he turned to his mother and his sister and the three of them embraced, tears of joy trickling down their cheeks.

Next, he sought out three of the most important men in his life: Ohio State coach Jim Tressel, Glenville High School coach Ted Ginn Sr., and OSU quarterbacks coach Joe Daniels, giving each of them a long hug.

"My heart was pounding. My mom could feel it when we hugged," said Smith. "She told me to calm down."

The Ohio State quarterback regained his composure and ascended the stairs to the podium, where Fowler, encircled by more than 20 former Heisman winners, was waiting. The 2006 Heisman Trophy was resting on a stand a few feet to their right.

Displaying a composure well beyond his years, but one that was hardly surprising given his coolness under fire on the football field, Smith, dressed in a gray pinstriped suit, delivered an eloquent acceptance speech during which he thanked his family, his teammates, and his coaches for the roles they had played in his development as both a young man and as a football player. That he did so without the benefit of any notes whatsoever was especially remarkable.

As ESPN was signing off the air, Fowler announced that Smith had received the highest percentage of first-place votes (86.7 percent) in Heisman Trophy history and also had accumulated the third highest point total of all time, behind the University of Southern California duo of O.J. Simpson and Reggie Bush. Smith had carried each of the six voting districts. McFadden, on the basis of a strong end-of-the-season showing, finished second, and Quinn, the Dublin, Ohio, native and high school star, third.

The voters across the country had confirmed what Ohio State fans had known all along: Troy Smith was indeed the best player in college football.

Smith became the first Big Ten quarterback since Ohio State's Les Horvath in 1944 to win the Heisman Trophy. He also is just the third African American quarterback to do so, joining Andre Ware of Houston in 1989 and Charlie Ward of Florida State in 1993.

When asked about those two distinctions, Smith said, "Given all the great quarterbacks that have played in the Big Ten, I am truly honored. With regard to the latter, I guess

Troy Smith became the seventh Buckeye to win the Heisman Trophy. Smith also took home the Walter Camp and Davey O'Brien Awards.

I will have to say this time and again in every interview that I do. I don't see color. I look at myself as a quarterback, not a black quarterback."

After accepting congratulations from many of the dignitaries fortunate enough to have secured tickets to the event, Smith spent the rest of the evening posing for pictures and doing countless interviews with the national media.

All three Columbus television stations had come to New York, and each of their sports anchors—Jeff Hogan of WBNS-TV, Clay Hall of WSYX-TV, and Jerod Smalley of WCMH-TV—was hoping for a live interview with the newly crowned Heisman Trophy winner.

Other members of the Ohio press corps included beat writers Tim May and Ken Gordon of the *Columbus Dispatch*, Marla Ridenour of the *Akron Beacon Journal*, Doug Harris of the *Dayton News*, Jason Lloyd of the *Lorain Morning Journal*, and Doug Lesmerises of the *Cleveland Plain Dealer*. Most had been in New York since Friday in an effort to get as much time as they could with Smith.

Finally, with the clock nearing the witching hour, a physically and emotionally drained Smith climbed into a limo and headed back to the hotel.

Sunday, December 10

Smith, Heisman Trophy in tow, appeared on *The NFL on CBS* and had a chance to spend time with two of the show's cohosts, James Brown and Dan Marino. The latter played his college football at Pittsburgh before going on to a Hall of Fame career in the NFL.

"We have something in common," said Marino. "Joe Daniels was my quarterbacks coach in college."

"I know," said Smith. "Your picture is in his office."

Smith left the CBS studio about 1:00 PM and headed back to the hotel. After more interviews (ESPN and Fox) and a tuxedo fitting in preparation for Monday night's formal dinner, he met with Rob Whalen and Tim Henning to review his itinerary for the rest of his stay in New York. Then it was back to his room to rest up before an evening dinner-dance for the former Heisman winners at a Battery Park restaurant.

The bus was scheduled to leave from the side entrance of the hotel at 6:15 PM.

"Don't be late," said Henning. "The old-timers can be hard on a rookie."

Troy flashed a smile and nodded his head as he headed to the elevators, hoping to elude the army of autograph seekers that was camped out in the hotel.

The ride to Battery Park down the West Side Highway took the group of football dignitaries past the old Downtown Athletic Club, the longtime home of the Heisman Memorial Trophy and a favorite gathering place for former Heisman winners until the catastrophic events of September 11, 2001. Now, the stately old building, which suffered

collateral damage in the attack, is being converted into con-
dominiums. Just past the DAC is Ground Zero. The bus was
eerily quiet for the next few minutes.

It was a clear night and as the Heisman winners, young
and old, entered the restaurant, the Statue of Liberty could
be seen in the distance.

During the course of the festive dinner that followed, Marcus
Allen, who was celebrating his 25th Heisman anniversary, and
Danny Wuerffel, who was celebrating his 10th, were feted.

Allen, who played for the University of Southern California, won the Heisman in 1981. A quarter of a century later,
the handsome and fit-looking running back gave every
appearance of still being able to play.

Wuerffel won his award in 1996, becoming the second
Heisman winner from the University of Florida. The first
was Steve Spurrier in 1966. The "old ball coach," as Spurrier
has since become known, was Wuerffel's coach at Florida,
the only time that a former Heisman recipient has coached a
current Heisman recipient.

One of the other finalists in 1996 was Ohio State offensive tackle Orlando Pace. Pace finished fourth that year as a
junior. He and fellow Buckeye John Hicks, who was second
in 1973, are the only two interior offensive linemen ever to
finish in the top four of the Heisman voting.

Wuerffel has been involved in humanitarian work since
leaving professional football. Two years ago, the Wuerffel

Trophy was established to honor a college football player who, in addition to excelling on the football field and in the classroom, takes an active role in humanitarian and faith-based efforts. Ohio State's Joel Penton was the 2006 Wuerffel Trophy winner.

Monday, December 11

Smith attended a breakfast honoring the top high school football players in the surrounding area. In the afternoon, he obligingly autographed more than 300 footballs and posters that will be used by the former Heisman winners for various charity events in which they are involved. Being a member of this exclusive Heisman fraternity does not come without a price. Smith was quickly realizing that.

The Heisman Dinner was held tonight at the Hilton. Nearly 2,000 dignitaries were in attendance at the black tie gala. The head table seated many of the former Heisman winners, including Johnny Lattner of Notre Dame, Pete Dawkins of Army, John Cappelletti of Penn State, and Mike Rozier of Nebraska.

Ohio State's Hopalong Cassady and Archie Griffin also were on the dais, as were university president Karen Holbrook, director of athletics Gene Smith, and Tressel.

The university also received permission from the Big Ten Conference to bring in Smith's three fellow cocaptains, center Doug Datish and defensive tackles Quinn Pitcock and David Patterson. They were seated at one of the four tables purchased by Ohio State.

It was a long but entertaining program and a once-in-a-lifetime event for the appreciative honoree.

"This has been a very, very, very, very long night," he said after being introduced by Tressel. "I know everyone is anxious to get home, but I want to thank the Heisman Trust and the voters for this very special award. To stand here in the presence of all this greatness is very humbling. I also want my cocaptains to know how very much it means to me to have you here tonight."

Tuesday, December 12

Smith returned to Columbus, where he faced yet another battery of reporters upon arrival at the airport. His life has changed. He is no longer Troy Smith, Ohio State quarterback. He has become Troy Smith, Heisman Trophy winner.

"How did I like New York?" he responded to one of the media questions at the airport. "It was crazy watching people drive. Lanes don't mean anything; every car is on an angle. And everyone is in a hurry, no matter what time of day. But I liked it and would like to go back."

He will. After all, he has a standing invitation every December from the Heisman Trust.

Smith, Pitcock, and Laurinaitis were all named to first-team berths on the Associated Press All-America team, and Ted Ginn Jr. was named to a second-team spot.

Wednesday, December 13

It was Troy Smith Day in Cleveland. Troy drove home this morning. During the ceremony in the gymnasium at Glenville High School, his former high school coach and longtime father figure, Ted Ginn Sr., announced the school was retiring Smith's No. 7 jersey.

The usually unflappable Smith had tears in his eyes as he thanked the crowd of well-wishers.

"When I think of the kids I grew up with who didn't make it out of here, I realize how blessed I am," he said. "I know that I could not have done the things I have done without the support of the people here."

"When I finish playing football, I hope to come back here and give back to this community in any way I can."

Smith drove back to Columbus following the ceremony. The Buckeyes have a practice scheduled for tomorrow morning.

Thursday, December 14

All hands were present and accounted for as the Buckeyes resumed practice. Finally, all the banquets are over and the players and coaches can get back to concentrating on football.

Troy Smith returned to Glenville High School in Cleveland to see his jersey retired in the days before the 2006 BCS National Championship Game.

Friday, December 15

Bowl media day. Players and coaches were available to local and national media. Smith and Tressel were the center of attention. A large number of media reps from Florida flew in for the session.

Tressel announced that juniors Antonio Pittman, Ted Ginn Jr., Anthony Gonzalez, and Kirk Barton have filed the appropriate documentation with the NFL to learn about their draft options in the spring. That would leave a huge hole offensively for the Buckeyes, who will already lose four senior starters.

Tuesday, December 19

Troy Smith was named Associated Press Player of the Year, collecting 59 of a possible 65 first-place votes. Darren McFadden and Hawaii quarterback Colt Brennan tied for second, each getting two votes. Brady Quinn was fourth, and West Virginia tailback Steve Slaton fifth.

Saturday, December 23

The team practiced in the morning and then headed home for Christmas.

Friday, December 29

The coaches and athletic administrators flew to Arizona. The team will stay in Fort McDowell until after the Fiesta

Bowl and then move into the Scottsdale Princess (where they have stayed in each of their last three trips to the Fiesta Bowl). Even though they are not required to be here until tomorrow, most of the players checked in by 6:00 PM local time.

Saturday, December 30

The first practice in Arizona.

Monday, January 1

Most of the team members and staff went to the Fiesta Bowl game, where Boise State upset heavily favored Oklahoma. Unfortunately, we left at the end of the third quarter and missed the miracle comeback.

Tuesday, January 2

Tressel went to the media hotel for a midmorning press conference that lasted about 30 minutes. Later in the day the team moved in at the Scottsdale Princess.

10

The BCS Championship Game

Sometimes a team, a really good team, just gets beat and there is simply no explanation. In a nutshell, that is exactly what happened to Ohio State in the 2006 national championship game in Glendale, Arizona.

After taking a 7–0 lead on Ted Ginn Jr.'s electrifying 93-yard kickoff return for a touchdown to open the game, the top-ranked Buckeyes fell to number two Florida by a final score of 41–14 in the BCS showdown.

The loss snapped the Buckeyes' 19-game winning streak and dashed their hopes of a second national championship in five years under Coach Tressel. It also ended a string of three consecutive bowl wins for Ohio State.

But on this night, before a sellout crowd of 74,628, more than half of which were there to cheer on their beloved Buckeyes, Florida was king of the desert.

If Ginn's spectacular return stunned college football fans, what happened during the next 59 minutes in University of Phoenix Stadium has put them in a state of shock. No team is unbeatable. But no one, absolutely no one, foresaw Florida dominating the Buckeyes.

Inexplicably, the high-powered Ohio State offense never got rolling against the Gators. The Buckeyes, who entered the game averaging 36 points and 409 yards per game, were held to 82 total yards and one offensive touchdown on 37 plays.

The OSU defense spent the night swimming upstream. The Gators, who repeatedly got the ball on the short side of the 50-yard line, made the most of their favorable field position by scoring 34 points on drives of 46 yards or less. Two of those scores followed costly personal foul penalties. Two others came after turnovers.

Florida led 34–14 at the half and had scored on drives of 46, 71, 32, six, and five yards. The Gators' lone score after halftime, which came in the fourth quarter, capped off a 39-yard drive.

The Chris Leak–led Gators scored on their first three possessions and were ahead 21–7 two plays into the second quarter.

The Buckeyes responded by moving 64 yards in four plays and cutting the lead to 21–14 on a nifty 18-yard run by tailback Antonio Pittman. A roughing-the-passer call on the first play of the drive, which was tacked on to the end of a 13-yard completion from Troy Smith to Brian Hartline, moved the ball to the Florida 36 and gave the Buckeyes

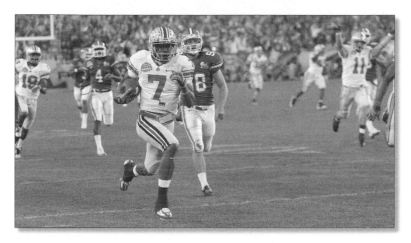

Ted Ginn Jr. returned the opening kickoff 93 yards for a Buckeyes touchdown in the 2007 BCS National Championship Game against Florida. Photo courtesy of Getty Images.

their best field position of the night. Really, it was their only good field position of the night. Pittman found pay dirt three plays later.

Now the defense needed a stop. They got it on the next series, forcing the Gators to punt. But the Buckeyes punted the ball right back to their Southeastern Conference foe and the Gators stretched the lead to 24–14 on a career-long 42-yard field goal by Chris Hetland.

With just over six minutes left in the first half, the Buckeyes took over at their own 20. A score here, either a touchdown or a field goal, would have given them a gigantic lift going into the locker room at halftime.

Four plays later, the Buckeyes found themselves facing a fourth-and-one at their own 29. Tressel, to the surprise of many, elected to roll the dice and go for it. It came up snake eyes. Beanie Wells, the 6'2", 230-pound freshman who throughout the course of the season had become OSU's short-yardage back, barreled into the line behind center Doug Datish and right guard T.J. Downing. He was stopped dead in his tracks. It was Florida's ball at the Buckeyes' 29-yard line.

"We needed to get something going," said Tressel afterward. "In the game of football, it oftentimes comes down to being able to make a yard when you need it and stopping the other team from making that same yard when they need it. We didn't do that."

Florida did not take advantage of its good fortune, however, and had to settle for a field goal and a 27–14 lead. It was still a two-touchdown game. The Buckeyes were still in it. Or so it seemed.

Unfortunately, this would turn out to be one of those games in which everything that can go wrong does. On the Buckeyes' next possession, Smith had the ball stripped from behind and the Gators recovered the loose pigskin at the Ohio State 5-yard line with 1:28 to play before intermission.

Three plays later the Gators took an insurmountable 34–14 lead on a one-yard pass from Tim Tebow to Andre Caldwell, who was all alone in the left corner of the end zone.

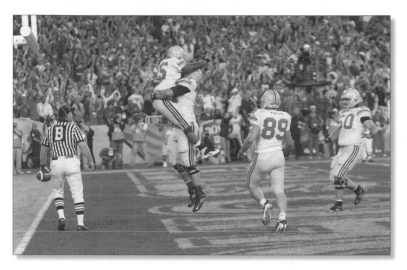

Ohio State fans erupted after running back Antonio Pittman scored a touchdown in the second quarter to cut the Gators' championship game lead to 21–14. Photo courtesy of Getty Images.

Tebow is the Gators' artful dodger, capable of stretching defenses with his athleticism. Florida coach Urban Meyer likes to bring his 6'3" freshman off the bench in short-yardage situations as a change of pace for Leak.

Ironically, the Buckeyes had gone into the championship game planning to employ Ginn in much the same way. But in the celebration following his touchdown on the opening play of the game, Teddy suffered a sprained ankle and missed the remainder of the game. One of the major weapons in the OSU offensive arsenal had been defused, unfortunately by friendly fire.

What Ginn would have done at quarterback is unknown, but his absence from the receiving corps certainly took the starch out of the Ohio State passing game and made it much easier for the Florida defense to exert pressure on Smith and the Buckeyes' offense.

The second half was pretty much a repeat of the first 30 minutes. The Gators seemed to have an answer for everything the Buckeyes tried, both offensively and defensively. The only scoring by either team was a one-yard run by Tebow with just over 10 minutes left in the game.

For the first time in four bowl trips to the Valley of the Sun, the Buckeyes would not be on the field for the victory celebration. As they headed to the locker room, fireworks went off and confetti filled the air. No one really noticed.

Following the game, Tressel talked to the team and thanked them for their effort during the year.

"We didn't get it done tonight and that is my fault," he told them. "But I am proud as can be of you, especially the seniors, and what you have accomplished this year."

After the required 10-minute cooling-off period, Tressel and his four cocaptains, Smith and Datish on offense and defensive tackles Quinn Pitcock and David Patterson, headed to their last postgame press conference as a group.

An hour later, the team was on its way back to the Scottsdale Fairmont Princess to meet with their families.

11

Moving Forward

Despite the shocking loss to the Gators, the sun did come up this morning. In fact, it was another beautiful day in Scottsdale with hardly a cloud in the sky and temperatures expected to reach the low 70s.

After breakfast at the hotel, the team and official party departed via charter for Columbus, arriving at Rickenbacker Airport late in the afternoon. As the players walked out of the terminal and boarded buses for the 15-minute ride back to campus, they were greeted by a small group of between 70 and 100 cheering fans who had braved the cold to show their support, win or lose, for the Buckeyes.

A few players did not return on the team plane. Five of them—Antonio Smith, Joel Penton, Roy Hall, Jay Richardson, and Justin Zwick—headed instead to Hawaii for next Saturday's Hula Bowl.

Troy Smith was scheduled to fly to Los Angeles to appear on Jay Leno's show Tuesday night if the Buckeyes won. Instead, he spent an extra day in Scottsdale before flying home.

Tressel and his wife, Ellen, flew to San Antonio on Monday afternoon for the American Football Coaches Association convention. Tressel is on the AFCA board of directors and is scheduled to speak to the group later in the week.

Thursday, January 11

Anthony Gonzalez met with the media to let them know he will forgo his senior year and enter the NFL draft. There was an early afternoon press conference in the team meeting room at the Woody Hayes Athletics Center.

With his parents, Eduardo and Jenna, in the back of the room, and a number of assistant coaches looking on, the emotional but poised receiver read a well-prepared statement and then took questions.

"This is one of the most difficult decisions of my life," said Gonzalez, an Academic All-American and a first-team All–Big Ten choice in 2006. "But I feel I am ready to take the next step in my life and fulfill my lifelong dream of playing in the NFL."

Gonzalez plans to enter law school after his football career is over and would like to one day become this country's first president of Hispanic descent. Judging by the way he fielded questions today, he will not be having any problems dealing with the media.

Friday, January 12

Tressel, who got back to town Thursday night, met with his staff to go over recruiting plans for the rest of the month.

Local talk-show hosts and columnists have spent the past four days speculating on what went wrong in the championship game. No one really seems to have a definitive answer, but there are lots of theories. Speculation on that subject will no doubt continue right up until the first game of the 2007 season.

When asked by Kirk Herbstreit on his afternoon talk show on WBNS Radio to put a finger on what happened in Glendale, Tressel replied, "As coaches, we didn't do a good enough job of getting the team ready. I don't think we were as mentally sharp as we could have been and that is my fault."

In his six years at Ohio State, Tressel has never blamed anyone but himself on those rare occasions when the Buckeyes have come up short. Interestingly, Tressel was born in 1952. Harry Truman was in office at the time. In true Truman fashion, the buck stops with Tressel when it comes to his team.

Monday, January 15

Pittman and Ginn Jr. announced they will go pro. Pittman made his announcement at his high school, Akron Buchtel, while the Ginn family issued a release through ESPN.com.

Ginn was the last to announce. His father, Ted Ginn Sr., admitted leaving Ohio State was not easy for his son even though the latter was virtually assured of being a high first-round pick in the upcoming NFL draft.

"There is something about being around Jim Tressel and being part of the Ohio State family," said Ginn Sr. "You don't want to leave."

Tuesday, February 6

Taver Johnson has joined the Ohio State staff as coach of the safeties and met with the media this afternoon. Johnson replaces Tim Beckman, who left OSU in February to become the offensive coordinator at Oklahoma State. Johnson, who has coached with current Ohio State coach John Peterson at Miami University (Ohio), is from Cincinnati. Peterson recommended him highly after Beckman moved on, but Johnson had just taken a job with the Oakland Raiders, so he appeared untouchable. Not so. When Jim Tressel called, Johnson quickly accepted.

Wednesday, February 7

National Signing Day. The loss of 19 seniors, including Heisman Trophy winner Troy Smith, and the early departure of three very talented juniors had the coaches sitting on the edge of their seats today. There were holes to fill. Sizeable holes.

Tressel and his staff responded by inking 15 of the nation's top high school prospects to national letters of intent on signing day. Fourteen of those recruits helped their teams advance to the playoffs in their respective state championships. The only signee who did not played on an undefeated team that was ineligible through no fault of his for playoff competition.

Tressel met with the media later to answer questions about the newest batch of Buckeyes.

"These guys know how to win," he said. "Best of all, they are excited to be Buckeyes and wear the Scarlet and Gray on Saturday afternoons in Ohio Stadium."

Ten of the recruits played their high school football in Ohio.

"Anytime you can sign 10 players from Ohio, you have a good nucleus to build on down the road," added the coach.

Tressel acknowledged one of this year's priorities was restocking the shelves with speed.

"Replacing the speed we lost was a high priority," he said. "We did that. We have some guys in this class who can run."

After spending just over an hour with the media, Tressel headed to the atrium of the Woody Hayes Athletics Center for his hour-long call-in radio show on WBNS. His departure allowed the press corps to spend the next 30 minutes with the assistant coaches. Eventually, the topic of conversation shifted from this year's recruiting class back to the national championship game. Coordinators Jim Bollman and Jim Heacock drew the biggest crowds.

"I am not sure I can explain what happened," said Bollman. "Why in the world, when we played well all year against some pretty good teams, would we not play well against Florida? I don't know. We haven't spent a lot of time yet looking at the films. We will do that, though, and try to learn from what happened."

Added Heacock, "We tried a lot of different things, but nothing seemed to work. The thing we have to do now is get back with our players and start getting ready for next year."

Tuesday, March 27

Tressel met with the media at the Woody Hayes Athletics Center to preview spring practice. Who the quarterback will be is the burning question. "If we had a game tomorrow, I would start Todd Boeckman," he replied. "But we don't, so I can use these 15 [spring] practices and the 29 next fall to get a more complete look at quarterback and every other position on our team."

Thursday, March 29

The Buckeyes opened spring practice.

Sunday, April 1

Tailback Beanie Wells sprained an ankle in practice and was ruled out for the remainder of spring ball.

Friday, April 6

The team held the first of two jersey scrimmages in Ohio Stadium. The offense came out on top and won the right to wear the home scarlet jerseys.

Todd Boeckman threw a pair of touchdown passes and Robby Schoenhoft had another. Defensive back Kurt Coleman reeled in two interceptions.

"Anyone who was there today [and it was closed to the media] knows we still have a long way to go," said Tressel afterward.

Saturday, April 14

Rain forced the second jersey scrimmage inside. This time the defense came out on top and won the right to wear the scarlet jerseys for the remainder of spring practice and into the fall. With the offensive line banged up (three projected starters out), Tressel turned up the heat and permitted more blitzing than normal. The defense collected four interceptions and recorded five sacks. Cornerback Donald Washington had two of the picks.

"We wanted to make life tougher for the quarterbacks today," said Tressel at the finish.

Wednesday, April 18

The team held its spring game draft. Tressel had previously divided the seniors into two teams. The Gray team won the toss and made junior defensive end Lawrence Wilson the first pick of the draft. The Scarlet seniors responded by choosing starting left tackle Alex Boone with their first pick. In one of the best moves of the day, the Scarlet players, which included quarterback Todd Boeckman, put their heads together and drafted Rob Schoenhoft, leaving the Gray team with inexperienced Antonio Henton as its only quarterback. Tressel intervened, however, decreeing that Schoenhoft would switch sides at halftime of Saturday's game.

Thursday, April 19

The Buckeyes held their kick scrimmage, which focuses on all aspects of special teams play, including the return game. Speedy sophomore-to-be Ray Small emerged as the leading contender to replace Ted Ginn Jr. as the Buckeyes' punt and kick return specialist. Like Ginn, Small played his high school ball at Glenville.

Saturday, April 21

Spring Game Day. At noon, judging from the 15,000 to 20,000 fans in Ohio Stadium, there was no way we would top last year's announced record crowd of 64,000. Last year we had everything going for us, including the return of Troy

Smith, Ted Ginn Jr., and Antonio Pittman and a seven-game winning streak that included back-to-back wins over Michigan and Notre Dame.

This team has been hit hard by graduation and lost the bowl game. Additionally, a number of marquee players, including tailback Chris Wells, were injured.

But by 12:30 PM the crowd had doubled. And at 1:00, just before kickoff, the stadium was full, except for the south stands, which were closed. It was a gorgeous day with temperatures hovering in the high 70s, and Ohio State fans were out in full force.

Shortly after the start of the second half, we announced the official attendance of 75,301, which might have been a wee bit on the conservative side. With a dollar from every ticket sold (tickets are $5 each) going either to the National Youth Sports Program or the Ronald McDonald House, everyone made out.

I guess I should not be surprised. After all, what better way is there to spend a Saturday afternoon, especially in Columbus, Ohio?

Appendix

Ohio State Football
2006 Game by Game Results

Game #1

Ohio State 35, Northern Illinois 12   9/2/06, Ohio Stadium

	1	2	3	4	F
NIU	0	3	3	6	12
OSU	21	7	0	7	35

First Quarter

OSU – Ginn Jr. 5 yd pass from T. Smith (Pettrey kick)	OSU 7	NIU 0
OSU – Ginn Jr. 58 yd pass from T. Smith (Pettrey kick)	OSU 14	NIU 0
OSU – Gonzalez 15 yd pass from T. Smith (Pettrey kick)	OSU 21	NIU 0

Second Quarter

OSU – Wells 8 yd run (Pettrey kick)	OSU 28	NIU 0
NIU – Nendick 35 yd FG	OSU 28	NIU 3

Third Quarter

NIU – Nendlck 37 yd FG	OSU 28	NIU 6

Fourth Quarter

OSU – Pittman 1 yd run (Pettrey kick)	OSU 35	NIU 6
NIU – Wolfe 4 yd pass from Horvath (rush failed)	OSU 35	NIU 12

Game #2

Ohio State 24, Texas 7   9/9/06, Royal–Texas Memorial Stadium

	1	2	3	4	F
OSU	7	7	3	7	24
TEX	0	7	0	0	7

First Quarter

OSU – Gonzalez 14 yd pass from T. Smith (Pettrey kick)	OSU 7	TEX 0

Second Quarter

TEX – Pittman 2 yd pass from McCoy (Johnson kick)	OSU 7	TEX 7
OSU – Ginn Jr. 29 yd pass from T. Smith (Pettrey kick)	OSU 14	TEX 7

Third Quarter

OSU – Pettrey 31 yd FG	OSU 17	TEX 7

Fourth Quarter

OSU – Pittman 2 yd run (Pettrey kick)	OSU 24	TEX 7

Game #3

Ohio State 37, Cincinnati 7   9/16/06, Ohio Stadium

	1	2	3	4	F
CIN	7	0	0	0	7
OSU	3	10	7	17	37

First Quarter

OSU – Pettrey 47 yd FG	OSU 3	CIN 0
CIN – Martin 22 yd pass from Grutza (Lovell kick)	CIN 7	OSU 3

Second Quarter

OSU – Pettrey 43 yd FG	CIN 7	OSU 6
OSU – Ginn Jr. 12 yd pass from T. Smith (Pettrey kick)	OSU 13	CIN 7

Third Quarter

OSU – Ginn Jr. 9 yd pass from T. Smith (Pettrey kick)	OSU 20	CIN 7

Fourth Quarter

OSU – Pittman 48 yd run (Pettrey kick)	OSU 27	CIN 7
OSU – Wells 9 yd run (Pettrey kick)	OSU 34	CIN 7
OSU – Pretorius 52 yd FG	OSU 37	CIN 7

Game #4

Ohio State 28, Penn State 6   9/23/06, Ohio Stadium

	1	2	3	4	F
PSU	0	3	0	3	6
OSU	0	0	7	21	28

First Quarter
No Scoring

Second Quarter
PSU – Kelly 21 yd FG   PSU 3   OSU 0

Third Quarter
OSU – Pittman 12 yd run (Pettrey kick)   OSU 7   PSU 3

Fourth Quarter
OSU – Robiskie 37 yd pass from T. Smith (Pettrey kick)   OSU 14   PSU 3
PSU – Kelly 23 yd FG   OSU 14   PSU 6
OSU – Jenkins 61 yd interception return (Pettrey kick)   OSU 21   PSU 6
OSU – A. Smith 55 yd interception return (Pretorius kick) OSU 28   PSU 6

Game #5

Ohio State 38, Iowa 17   9/30/06, Kinnick Stadium

	1	2	3	4	F
OSU	7	14	7	10	38
IOWA	3	7	0	7	17

First Quarter
OSU – Gonzalez 12 yd pass from T. Smith (Pettrey kick)   OSU 7   IOWA 0
IOWA – Schlicher 32 yd FG   OSU 7   IOWA 3

Second Quarter
OSU – Pittman 4 yd run (Petty kick)   OSU 14   IOWA 3
IOWA – Young 15 yd run (Schlicher kick)   OSU 14   IOWA 10
OSU – Hall 6 yd pass from T. Smith (Pettrey kick)   OSU 21   IOWA 10

Third Quarter
OSU – Gonzalez 30 yd pass from T. Smith (Pettrey kick)   OSU 28   IOWA 10

Fourth Quarter
OSU – Pettrey 36 yd FG   OSU 31   IOWA 10
IOWA – Brodell 4 yd pass from Tate (Schlicher kick)   OSU 31   IOWA 17
OSU – Robiskie 12 yd pass from T. Smith (Pettrey kick)   OSU 38   IOWA 17

Game #6

Ohio State 35, Bowling Green 7   10/7/06, Ohio Stadium

	1	2	3	4	F
BG	0	0	7	0	7
OSU	14	7	0	14	35

First Quarter
OSU – Nichol 3 yd pass from T. Smith (Pettrey kick)   OSU 7   BG 0
OSU – Pittman 8 yd run (Pettrey kick)   OSU 14   BG 0

Second Quarter
OSU – Pittman 8 yd run (Pettrey kick)   OSU 21   BG 0

Third Quarter
BG – Partridge 12 yd pass from Turner (Ellis kick)   OSU 21   BG 7

Fourth Quarter
OSU – Small 11 yd pass from T. Smith (Pettrey kick)   OSU 28   BG 7
OSU – Ginn Jr. 57 yd pass from T. Smith (Pettrey kick)   OSU 35   BG 7

Game #7

Ohio State 38, Michigan State 7   10/14/06, Spartan Stadium

	1	2	3	4	F
OSU	7	17	7	7	38
MSU	0	0	0	7	7

First Quarter
OSU – Pittman 2 yd run (Pettrey kick)   OSU 7   MSU 0

Second Quarter
OSU – Pettrey 32 yd FG   OSU 10   MSU 0
OSU – Ginn Jr. 60 yd punt return (Pettrey kick)   OSU 17   MSU 0
OSU – Gonzalez 12 yd pass from T. Smith (Pettrey kick)   OSU 24   MSU 0

Third Quarter
OSU – Robiskie 7 yd pass from T. Smith (Pettrey kick)   OSU 31   MSU 0

Fourth Quarter
OSU – Wells 5 yd run (Pettrey kick)   OSU 38   MSU 0
MSU – Jimmerson 6 yd run (Swenson kick)   OSU 38   MSU 7

Game #8

Ohio State 44, Indiana 3   10/21/06, Ohio Stadium

	1	2	3	4	F
IND	3	0	0	0	3
OSU	7	21	10	6	44

First Quarter
IND – Starr 34 yd FG	IND 3	OSU 0
OSU – Nichol 23 yd pass from T. Smith (Pettrey kick)	OSU 7	IND 3

Second Quarter
OSU – Ginn Jr.31 yd pass from T. Smith (Pettrey kick)	OSU 14	IND 3
OSU – Gonzalez 5 yd pass from T. Smith (Pettrey kick)	OSU 21	IND 3
OSU – Ballard 1 yd pass from T. Smith (Pettrey kick)	OSU 28	IND 3

Third Quarter
OSU – Nichol 38 yd pass from Ginn Jr. (Pettrey kick)	OSU 35	IND 3
OSU – Pettrey 51 yd FG	OSU 38	IND 3

Fourth Quarter
OSU – Wells 12 yd run (kick failed)	OSU 44	IND 3

Game #9

Ohio State 44, Minnesota 0   10/28/06, Ohio Stadium

	1	2	3	4	F
MIN	0	0	0	0	0
OSU	10	7	13	14	44

First Quarter
OSU – Pittman 10 yd run (Pettrey kick)	OSU 7	MIN 0
OSU – Pettrey 42 yd FG	OSU 10	MIN 0

Second Quarter
OSU – Robiskie 18 yd pass from T. Smith (Pettrey kick)	OSU 17	MIN 0

Third Quarter
OSU – T. Smith 21 yd run (Pettrey kick)	OSU 24	MIN 0
OSU – Pittman 13 yd run (kick blocked)	OSU 30	MIN 0

Fourth Quarter
OSU – Wells 3 yd run (Pettrey kick)	OSU 37	MIN 0
OSU – Zwick 1 yd run (Pettrey kick)	OSU 44	MIN 0

Game #10

Ohio State 17, Illinois 10   11/4/06, Memorial Stadium

	1	2	3	4	F
OSU	7	10	0	0	17
ILL	0	0	0	10	10

First Quarter
OSU – Wells 2 yd run (Pettrey kick)   OSU 7   ILL 0

Second Quarter
OSU – Pittman 1 yd run (Pettrey kick)   OSU 14   ILL 0
OSU – Pettrey 50 yd FG   OSU 17   ILL 0

Third Quarter
No Scoring

Fourth Quarter
ILL – Reda 27 yd FG   OSU 17   ILL 3
ILL – Mendenhall 3 yd run   OSU 17   ILL 10

Game #11

Ohio State 54, Northwestern 10   11/11/06, Ryan Field

	1	2	3	4	F
OSU	21	12	14	7	54
NW	0	10	0	0	10

First Quarter
OSU – Hartline 14 yd pass from T. Smith (Pettrey kick)   OSU 7   NW 0
OSU – Pittman 1 yd run (Pettrey kick)   OSU 14   NW 0
OSU – Mitchell 46 yd interception return (Pettrey kick)   OSU 21   NW 0

Second Quarter
NW – Howells 29 yd FG   OSU 21   NW 3
OSU – Hartline 9 yd pass from T. Smith (kick blocked)   OSU 27   NW 3
NW – Sutton 8 yd pass from Bacher (Howells kick)   OSU 27   NW 10
OSU – Ginn Jr. 34 pass from T. Smith (run failed)   OSU 33   NW 10

Third Quarter
OSU – Gonzalez 6 yd pass from T. Smith (Pettrey kick)   OSU 40   NW 10
OSU – Wells 1 yd run (Pettrey kick)   OSU 47   NW 10

Fourth Quarter
OSU – Boeckman 4 yd run (Pretorius kick)   OSU 54   NW 10

Game #12

Ohio State 42, Michigan 39   11/18/06, Ohio Stadium

	1	2	3	4	F
MICH	7	7	10	15	39
OSU	7	21	7	7	42

First Quarter

MICH – Hart 1 yd run (Rivas kick)	MICH 7	OSU 0
OSU – Hall 1 yd pass from T. Smith (Pettrey kick)	OSU 7	MICH 7

Second Quarter

OSU – Wells 52 yd run (Pettrey kick)	OSU 14	MICH 7
OSU – Ginn, Jr. 39 yd pass from Smith (Pettrey kick)	OSU 21	MICH 7
MICH – Arrington 37 yd pass from Henne (Rivas kick)	OSU 21	MICH 14
OSU – Gonzalez 8 yd pass from Smith (Pettrey kick)	OSU 28	MICH 14

Third Quarter

MICH – Hart 2 yd run (Rivas kick)	OSU 28	MICH 21
MICH – Rivas 39 yd field goal	OSU 28	MICH 24
OSU – Pittman, 56 yd run (Pettrey kick)	OSU 35	MICH 24

Fourth Quarter

MICH – Hart 1 yd run (Rivas kick)	OSU 35	MICH 31
OSU – Robiskie 13 yd pass from T. Smith (Pettrey kick)	OSU 42	MICH 31
MICH – Ecker 16 yd pass from Henne (Breaston pass from Henne)	OSU 42	MICH 39

Game #13

Florida 41, Ohio State 14   1/7/07, University of Phoenix Stadium,
                                   BCS National Championship Game

	1	2	3	4	F
FLA	14	20	0	7	41
OSU	7	7	0	0	14

First Quarter

OSU – Ginn Jr. 93 yd kickoff return (Pettrey kick)	OSU 7	FLA 0
FLA – Baker 14 yd pass from Leak (Hetland kick)	OSU 7	FLA 7
FLA – Harvin 4 run (Hetland kick)	FLA 14	OSU 7

Second Quarter

FLA – Wynn 2 yd run (Hetland kick)	FLA 21	OSU 7
OSU – Pittman 18 yd run (Pettrey kick)	FLA 21	OSU 14
FLA – Hetland 42 yd FG	FLA 24	OSU 14
FLA – Hetland 40 yd FG	FLA 27	OSU 14
FLA – Caldwell 1 yd pass from Tebow (Hetland kick)	FLA 34	OSU 14

Third Quarter

No Scoring

Fourth Quarter

FLA – Tebow 1 yd run (Hetland kick)	FLA 41	OSU 14